THE EMPEROR'S PANDA

T·H·E
EMPEROR'S
PANDA

by DAVID DAY

Illustrated by ERIC BEDDOWS

Dodd, Mead & Company
New York

1   2   3   4   5   6   7   8   9   10

Library of Congress Cataloging-in-Publication Data

Day, David, date
The emperor's panda.

Summary: Relates how the poor young shepherd boy
Kung became the Emperor of all China with the help of the
Master Panda, the most magical and wisest creature in all
the world.
[1. Pandas—Fiction. 2. Magic—Fiction. 3. China—
Fiction] I. Beddows, Eric, date ill. II. Title.
PZ7.D3294Em   1986   [Fic]   86-32818
ISBN 0-396-09036-2

Originally published in Canada by
McClelland and Stewart Limited, Toronto, 1986
Designed by Esther Pflug

For my daughter,
TAROT

Also by David Day

Contents

The Land of Sung Wu

I F YOU LOOK at a map of China today, I'm afraid you will never find the land of Sung Wu, but I promise you in the ancient days of the Celestial Empire it did exist. And indeed it was famous. Not because it was such a wondrous place, for in those days there were many strange and wonderful things in the world. Sung Wu was just another slightly enchanted realm to be found along the legendary Silk Road of the West which led to the Imperial City. Like many other lands, Sung Wu was inhabited by its share of bandits and peasants, a few monsters and lesser demons, a hypnotizing ogre here, a spring of forgetfulness there. But these things, of course, were no reason for real fame. No, Sung Wu became famous because a poor orphan boy called Kung the Fluteplayer lived there, and because Kung went on a great adventure that changed the destiny of the whole empire.

On its western border Sung Wu was bypassed by the majestic silk caravans, and its people were mostly poor and humble folk who earned meagre livings as herdsmen, woodcutters and herb gatherers. They knew little of the world beyond Sung Wu, and knew nothing of the extravagance and power of the Imperial City that lay at the end of the Silk Road.

Yet occasionally travellers did pass through Sung Wu and they told of the wonders of the world beyond. Then the people listened to their tales in amazement and gave the travellers what little food and shelter they possessed.

One morning Kung the Fluteplayer was sitting on a hillock while his sheep grazed about him. From his belt he took his bamboo flute and began to play. It was a beautiful spring day and the meadows were lush and green. Kung's spirit soared in the sunlight while the sound of his flute echoed and danced over the hills.

Kung lived with his uncle, Latzu, in the eastern part of Sung Wu. Here the borders were defined by the double barrier of the dense bamboo forests of the Enchanted Valley and the rugged and impassable Dharka Mountains. Kung and his uncle were happy in their humble way and earned a modest living herding the blue mountain sheep of Sung Wu.

Uncle Latzu was a good man with a gentle and compassionate nature. He had cared for the orphaned Kung since he was a baby, and Kung grew into a dutiful and loving nephew. He was a sensitive boy, loyal and even-tempered.

Latzu believed he could discern a special talent in Kung, and when the boy was very young Latzu went to the forests of the Enchanted Valley. From the forest bamboo he carved a beautiful flute for his nephew. This proved the finest of all possible gifts because Kung did indeed have a considerable talent. No one ever needed to teach him how to play the flute. He learned by listening to the breath of

the wind as it moved over hill and plain or through the grasses and the trees.

When Kung played his flute on the hills and the sound carried down to the paths and roadways, folk who were travelling would stop and listen a while, then go on, feeling happier for having heard Kung's haunting music. And his sheep would follow him, entranced and content.

On this particular day Kung was staring down the valley to where the dirt road wound its way out of the west. In the distance he saw three travellers. Gradually they approached and turned up the path leading to his uncle's cottage. Half an hour later the travellers were near enough for Kung to see them clearly. They were the strangest men he had ever encountered.

They wore black cloaks that Kung had only seen before on the good monks who came out of the monastery fortresses of the Forbidden Mountains. But these men were different. Like the rich merchants of the Silk Road, they wore bright jewels and strange amulets; and like the soldiers of the Emperor, they were armoured and armed. One carried a massive sword, another a spear, and the third a long bow. Each wore a broad black belt studded with silver and the forearms of each man were covered with armguards, again black and studded with silver. In each belt a broad dagger was thrust, with a handle like a griffon head.

The Bowman, who had his hood thrown back, had pale yellow skin like Kung's, but Kung believed he must be one of the tribesmen of the northern barbarian people. His appearance was much as Kung had heard other folk speak of. The Bowman had a long thin moustache that drooped down either side of his mouth. His head was shaved, except for a long topknot like a horse's tail, and his eyes were quick and black like a hawk's.

The Spearman was a brown-skinned man from the southern realms of Cimia. His straight black hair fit like a helmet, except for two long braids that hung down either side of his tattooed face. He used his spear as a staff, and there was something elegant and cat-like in the rhythm of his walk.

But the Swordsman was the strangest of the three travellers. Kung had heard tales of a land at the western end of the Silk Road where the sun falls boiling into the farthest ocean. There, they claimed, the white-skinned men lived. But this man had not only white skin but yellow hair and blue eyes! And he wore a headband set with a stone the same blue as his eyes.

Kung continued playing his flute, so when the Swordsman was near enough, he looked up at Kung on his hillock. The sun glinted on the blue stone over his forehead, and when he saw the source of the music, he smiled and waved. Then the travellers looked back to their path and soon followed the track toward the cottage of Kung's uncle.

That evening when Kung returned to his home he found that Uncle Latzu had made the travellers his guests. The Spearman, whose name was Tamba, was a mute. The Bowman, Tu, could speak, but like most northern tribesmen, he was a man of few words. It was Toran the Swordsman who spoke eloquently for all three. He told of the great cities and bazaars along the caravan road and of their own perilous journey before they even reached the Silk Road. He described how they were set upon by bandits, nearly drowned in a sudden flood, and then later almost perished for lack of water in a great desert. But most of all Kung and his uncle wished to hear of the place Toran and his companions had travelled from—the Forbidden Mountains, the highest and greatest mountains on earth.

They had come, Toran claimed, from the monastery fortresses of Lhasa in the Forbidden Mountains. They were guardsmen and servants of those excellent men in that sacred place. Indeed, it was on their masters' behalf that they had set out on this journey, for they had an urgent message for the Emperor, which was to reach the Imperial City by the Festival of the Moon.

Fourteen days remained in which to reach their destination. They could only do so by taking an ancient road that once ran directly through the heart of Sung Wu and through a secret pass in the Dharka Mountains.

Kung's uncle looked at the three travellers with astonishment. Latzu was an old and wise man, one of the few who knew the secret pass existed.

"Surely," he said, "if you know of the secret pass, you know that such a journey is impossible. First there is the Enchanted Valley, which many folk call the Sleeping Bamboo, and from which so many have failed to return. And even if you made your way through the Enchanted Valley without falling under its spell, you would be in even greater danger in the pass. You must know that in ancient times this was called the Pass of the Ice Dragon because of the monster that is its guardian. I know of none who have ever managed that journey."

"My good Latzu," said Toran the Swordsman, smiling and looking on the old man with his cool blue eyes. "Of all this we are well aware, but our duty is clear. We must attempt the journey. The Holy Men of the Forbidden Mountains have given us certain powers. However, we are in need of help, and for this we have come to you, my honourable Latzu. You are among the few men of Sung Wu who have entered the Enchanted Valley and returned. You alone can guide us through its intricate pathways to the entrance of the Dragon Pass."

Kung looked at his uncle in astonishment, for even he did not know that Latzu had intimate knowledge of the Enchanted Valley.

"You arc brave men to attempt such a journey," said Latzu. He sat quietly for a moment, looking into the firelight. "But as you are emissaries of the Holy Men of the Forbidden Mountains, and as I am bound to serve my Emperor, I will guide you to the gate of the pass."

"The blessings of the Nine Heavens are upon you, my good Latzu!" the Swordsman said with a flourish. The three travellers raised their cups and drank in salute. But Toran could still read the look of concern on Latzu's face, and Tu the Bowman gave the Swordsman a darting glance with his hawkish black eyes.

"Fear not for us, Latzu," said Toran, "for we are well protected. We will pass without danger. We need only one who knows the paths of the Enchanted Valley. Once at the entrance to the Dragon Pass, we alone will confront the Ice Dragon. And from the far side of the pass to the Imperial City is only a journey of six days. Thus we will reach the Emperor before the Festival of the Moon."

The next morning Kung watched his uncle lead the three travellers down the winding trails and into the Enchanted Valley.

The Enchanted Valley

K UNG'S UNCLE did not return on the third day, as he had promised, nor on the fourth. Kung believed his uncle and the travellers had fallen into serious trouble. On the fourth day he went to fetch a cousin to tend to his sheep, then he packed a little food, his flute and the three copper coins that were all his wealth, and resolved that he would leave the next morning to search for his uncle.

On the fifth morning after Latzu's departure, Kung was travelling on the eastward trail toward the Enchanted Valley. In a very short time he was at the edge of the forest of Sleeping Bamboo. There Kung took a deep breath and plunged into the dense bamboo forest and stepped onto one of its thousand trails. Though fearful of this valley that so many had entered and few had left, Kung bravely went on in search of his uncle.

The forest was dark and dense with huge bamboos and many strange and beautiful trees. Yet it did not seem a fearful place. Birds sang gentle songs, the wind sighed through rustling branches. There were huge blossoming rhododendrons and crimson trunked asoka trees showering golden petals. Drunken black bees hummed from the sweet kokila to the coral flower and the air was heavy with the scent of honeyflower and mango. The songs of the mimicking sarika birds mingled with the sounds of the valley's many clear-running brooks. It was a place of gentleness and contentment.

As Kung went on he saw the power of the forest of Sleeping Bamboo. On one trail he came upon three silk merchants in costly robes and jewels. They sat propped up against a large tree by the trail, as if they had stopped to rest. But when Kung attempted to wake them, he found that he could not. The gentleness of the forest had rocked them into a deep trance, and the lullaby of the wind in the bamboo had put them to sleep forever.

Farther along Kung came upon fierce soldiers and warriors armed with swords and halberds, vagabonds in rags and haughty women in silken gowns attended by ladies-in-waiting. In one place he found a king from the south with a huge ruby in his turban, and a thief with the King's purse overtaken by sleep in mid-flight.

Some were sitting, some lying, some propped against trees; all were sleeping peacefully. Vine leaves and flowers had grown around them and tendrils twined about their arms and through their hair. Squirrels had made a home in one soldier's helmet held under his arm. A beautiful maiden in a silk dress and velvet cape had a family of parakeets in a nest in her hair. Yet otherwise all were unhurt and untouched by anything evil, and all wore expressions of happiness in their deep sleep.

Kung soon came to believe that the source of the valley's enchantment was not evil, but he feared this spirit that folk called the Master of the Sleeping Bamboo, for he had no wish to remain here forever. So although he did not feel in the least sleepy, Kung kept pinching himself lest he join the others in their eternal dream.

On and on went Kung, deeper into the bamboo forest. First he went one way, then another, but often he returned to a sleeping king or a slumbering maiden he had passed many hours before. In the impossible maze of trails, he lost his way time and again and came around in a circle. Finally, as evening was approaching, Kung saw a faint light ahead and soon found himself on the bank of a small stream. The water was filled with the glimmering light of the setting sun.

Kung sat down on the bank and leaned against a tree to rest. He had nearly exhausted himself with his wanderings and he was very tired. From his sack he took some pieces of fruit and a rice cake to make himself a small meal.

As the sun set, Kung watched the patterns of light playing on the dark trunks, stalks and limbs of the forest. The bamboo swayed gently, rippling like water. Kung was becoming drowsy. The birds sang softly, the wind sighed. And Kung drifted into a deep sleep.

When Kung opened his eyes, it was no longer evening. The full light of the morning sun shone on his face. He seemed to be in the same place where he had fallen asleep, yet when he looked across the stream to the other bank, he was sure that he was dreaming.

At the foot of a tree across the stream was a large furry black-and-white creature chewing on a bamboo stalk. And although Kung had never seen such a creature before, he knew exactly what it was; just as you or I would know exactly what a dragon or a griffon was, even if we hadn't seen one before. For in ancient China there was only *one* Panda in all the world, and he was the rarest, most magical

19

and wisest of all creatures in creation. He was called Lord Beishung, the Master Panda.

Legends told how the Supreme-Being-of-the-Ninth-Heaven created the Panda before He even made the world, and how the Panda advised Him in the shaping of all things under the heavens. When this work was done, the Supreme Being sent the Panda into the court of the master of the world, the Emperor of China.

Through many ages and dynasties the Panda advised in the emperors' courts, but one day, over a thousand years ago, he went out for a walk in the imperial gardens and was never seen again. Many believed the Master Panda had returned to the Ninth Heaven.

So the sight of the Panda munching on a bamboo stalk across the clearing from Kung was enough to convince the boy that this was all a dream. He was even more convinced when he saw the Panda's bright eyes settling on him and a deep but gentle voice came from the bear-like creature. "Good morning, young Kung."

Kung was so astonished, he could not make even a polite reply, but instead pinched himself very, very hard. "Ouch!" he yelped.

But the Panda did not disappear. Instead, he got up on all fours and waded through the stream until he was standing right in front of the speechless Kung.

"Now, now, young man," said Panda, "don't do yourself an injury. Let me assure you that you are not sleeping *and* you are under no spell. I am Lord Beishung, the Panda. I assume you've heard of me, even though my deeds have been half forgotten in the past centuries. Is that so?"

Kung sat with his mouth hanging open, but nodded his head.

"Yes, well, so you have," said the Master Panda, flopping down on his hindquarters. "But unknown to most folk of the world, for the past . . . oh, ten centuries or so I've made my home here in the Sleeping Bamboo. Such a tranquil place, don't you think?"

Again Kung nodded.

"Ah, yes." Panda sat with one paw propping up his chin. "Well, you seem a little speechless this morning. Won't you play your flute for me, my young friend?"

Clearing his throat and moistening his lips, the awestruck Kung began to play for that rarest and most magical of beasts, the Master Panda. And once he began to play his flute, all his shyness left him. The music took over and its melodies blended with the wind in the bamboo, and it seemed the forest swayed in rhythm and the birds came down and sang as a chorus.

LORD BEISHUNG

AFTER SOME TIME, as Kung came toward the end of a melody, the Panda raised his paw. "Thank you, little Fluteplayer, for the pleasure you give! Now come breakfast with me."

The Panda held out a paw, then turned it to reveal a tangerine. As he juggled it to his other paw, two tangerines appeared. Then two apples, three plums, a peach, two pomegranates and a grapefruit!

"Little juggling and conjuring tricks I picked up to entertain the nobles in the court in the old days," Panda explained to the amazed Kung.

Panda piled all the fruit on his lap, then appeared to take a large silk napkin out of his right ear. He spread the napkin like a picnic cloth between Kung and himself, and carefully placed the fruit on the cloth. With another sleight of paw, Panda produced a few small honeyed rice cakes and a mound of nuts and raisins.

After a paw-waving signal that invited Kung to begin, both fell hungrily on their breakfasts. Munching into an apple while clutching a half-eaten honeyed rice cake, Kung began to feel more relaxed.

"My ... my Lord Beishung," he said, "I beg to ask how the honourable Panda knows my name."

"My young Kung," replied Panda, scratching his ear with a bamboo stalk and holding a piece of pomegranate, "I have known of you for many years. I have listened as you played to your flocks on the hills above the Enchanted Valley. With your flute you have gained a wisdom that many an ancient man never achieves."

"I am honoured by your fine words, my Lord Beishung," said Kung rather hesitantly, "but surely I am not worthy. I know nothing of music. My teachers have only been the wind in the grass and the bamboo."

"Not one in ten thousand has the wisdom and humility to learn so simple a lesson," remarked the Panda. "For as *The Book of the Sages* says, 'The wind is to the earth as the soul is to the body.' You may take my word on these matters, Kung. You see, I am the essence of balance!" proclaimed Panda rather grandly while standing upside-down on one forepaw. Then he cartwheeled right over to the other forepaw, then back again, then forward into a ball, then he emerged again in a sitting position directly in front of Kung!

"In all ways I am balanced, as the colour of my coat must show." He pointed to various parts of his body and head. "I am equal parts black and white, as you can see. And when the Supreme-Being-of-the-Ninth-Heaven shaped the earth out of disorder and chaos, it was I who was at His side. And I must tell you, Kung, it was a marvellous thing. The most marvellous thing."

Panda pondered a moment, then he chuckled. "The

23

Wise Clown, He sometimes called me, or the Harlequin Bear. And I would dance for Him. I would juggle. I would roll over, do a cartwheel and roll in a ball."

The Panda went through his tumbling routine as Kung swallowed the last of his apple.

"Ah, those were grand days. Taming the world, balancing things out. Light and Darkness. Fire and Ice. Air and Water.... Then after the world was made and all the animals and people and plants were put on the earth, we watched from the Ninth Heaven. And for a good long while everything was well enough, but then you humans began running things. That was when the Supreme Being turned to me. 'Panda,' He said, 'you'll have to go down there and give some advice. Otherwise, we'll be back to chaos in no time.'

"That's when He sent me down into the Emperor of China's court," said Panda, swallowing a plum. "It seems that all rulers need to be reminded from time to time of the most basic principle of life under the Nine Heavens. Without balance, nothing survives, certainly not an empire. So there I was for ever so long in the emperors' courts, tumbling and balancing and advising, just as I had done in the Ninth Heaven. And every now and then an emperor would come to me and say, 'Ah, yes, blessings upon you, Most-Excellent-Lord-Beishung-the-Master-Panda. That is exactly what is needed – not war, not violence, but balance.' And so order was restored and China became a land of peace."

Panda looked down at the napkin and the relative chaos of the scattered remains of the breakfast. He saw that Kung had stopped eating some time ago, so he scooped up one last pawful of nuts and tossed it in his mouth.

Enjoying Kung's interest in his conjuring tricks, Panda chuckled, then tucked the silk napkin back into the same ear he had taken it from at the beginning of the meal.

MASTER OF THE SLEEPING BAMBOO

"**N**OW, YOUNG MAN," said Panda, clearing his throat and getting onto all four feet, "we must be on our way in haste or you'll never rescue your Uncle Latzu, will you?"

It was as if the Panda had been reading Kung's mind.

"You know my Uncle Latzu? Have you seen him? What has happened to him? Can you help me...."

"Now, now, one question at a time," said the Panda calmly. "But let us walk as we talk. We have a long way to go and it's best not to waste time."

The Panda and the boy walked side by side along a path that led deep into the bamboo forest.

"As to your first question, Kung: Yes, I know your Uncle Latzu. We have been good friends for many years. Living nearby, he visits me often – though he has kept my presence here a secret."

"My most honourable Lord," pleaded Kung, "tell me what news you have of him. I am dreadfully afraid that, like many others, he has been caught under some powerful spell in this valley." Looking around the forest in case they were being overheard, Kung whispered, "I think it must be the spirit called the Master of the Sleeping Bamboo."

Panda looked at Kung in a rather curious way. As he walked on, he chuckled to himself. Then he cleared his throat. "I'm sorry, Kung, it is not your distress that amuses me. Indeed, this is a serious matter. However, I must assure you that the good Latzu is not under the spell of the Sleeping Bamboo. You see, my young friend, *I* am the Master of the Sleeping Bamboo."

Panda ambled along the winding path while Kung tried to regain his wits and catch up with him.

"As you can see, here in my valley there is peace – and of that I am master," said the Panda. "Not of great armies, not of demons, not of monsters with horrible powers. The spell of the Sleeping Bamboo will harm no one, but anyone with evil or corruption will fall into an enchanted sleep. The sleep is a deep healing remedy to the soul, and the body does not age a single day, though the sleeper may stay within the forest for two hundred years."

"Can they never be released from this sleep?" Kung asked with great concern.

"Most certainly," said Panda, rather surprised at the question. "The sleep is no punishment. I don't believe in punishment. They simply remain until the balance of their true nature is restored. When that has occurred and they are again balanced and wholesome, the spell falls from them. Then they emerge from the Sleeping Bamboo as innocent and good as newborn children."

At this point the forest trail emerged on one side of a high rocky gorge. From there a fallen tree bridged the thirty-foot gap over the gorge. Kung looked at the narrow-

ness of the tree trunk, then peered down into the deep chasm below. The prospect of the crossing made him gulp.

"Come, come, now," said Panda, "no time for loitering. Just hop onto my back, grip the fur on my neck and we'll nip over the gorge in no time. The Master of Balance is not likely to fall off a log, now is he?"

And so Kung did exactly as he was told and soon found himself clinging to Panda's hair as they teetered along over the high gorge. Panda said it would just take a minute to cross – it seemed a very long minute to Kung. Seeing the river wavering far below them, Kung decided to close his eyes, until he felt Panda's feet scuff along on the earth again. "As a rule," explained Panda, "it is only babes and Holy Men of the Forbidden Mountains who can pass through the Sleeping Bamboo without falling under its spell."

"Then why is it that I have not fallen under its spell?" asked Kung.

"Have I not told you that you are one in ten thousand? You have listened to the wind and with your flute have learned the great lesson. You are filled with an inner peace which allows you to walk in my realm without fear of falling under its spell. It has been a long time since one such as you has entered the Sleeping Bamboo. Even your Uncle Latzu, good man that he is, when he entered the Bamboo as a young man, slept for two full years."

"So now my uncle can walk here freely as well," said Kung. "But tell me, my Lord, is there another spirit in this forest that has captured him?"

"No power has held him here in my valley. But I'm afraid I was unable to help him."

"Is he in trouble? Are the three travellers with him also in danger?"

"I'm sorry to say, my young Kung, that the three travellers with him *are* the trouble!" Panda paused rather thoughtfully. "They are not what they seemed. They are not pilgrims or messengers. They are folk out of that hot desert land of sorcerers called Zandu which lies beyond the Forbidden Mountains."

"But they told us they were the guardians and messengers of the Holy Men of the Forbidden Mountains," said a shocked Kung. "They said they must travel through the Enchanted Valley and the Dragon Pass to reach the Imperial City with a message for the Emperor before the Festival of the Moon."

"I'm afraid," said Panda sympathetically, "that wizards are master deceivers. The Holy Men have no soldiers or guardsmen and they carry their own messages."

"But how did such evil men manage to pass through the Sleeping Bamboo without falling under its spell?" asked Kung, who was dreadfully upset at the thought of his uncle in such company.

"Unfortunately," said Panda, "all three possess shadow rings. These are wizards' gold rings that protect the wearers from the enchantments of others. Many wizards wear these rings to protect them from spells they cast on each other. However, they also protect them from my particular enchantments. Still, they would have become lost in the maze of trails in the Sleeping Bamboo if your uncle had not guided them through."

"Then they have taken Uncle Latzu into the Pass of the Ice Dragon!" exclaimed the alarmed Kung. "But why would they wish to take him there? Indeed, why would they go into that pass if their story is untrue?"

"These men are not mere wizards. They are among the few in the world who might truly be called dragon fighters. And this is the reason for their desire to enter the Dragon Pass."

The path led into a clearing with a stream that fell over a rock bluff in a dozen little rivulets and into a deep pool enclosed by large round stones and green ferns. Three cedar trees stood in the clearing near the pool. While Kung drank deeply of the cold water, Panda flopped down on his hindquarters and soaked his back paws in the pool.

Hundreds of brilliantly coloured fishes moved like shimmering lights beneath the water. Some came up to

Panda's paws. They ran their purple or gold or scarlet finny backs along his soles, daring to tickle the toes of the great Lord Beishung.

"My Lord," said Kung, interrupting the Panda's playful communication with his finny friends, "why would the wizards dare to fight an Ice Dragon?"

"There is much these men would risk because of their greed. You see, ice dragons possess a great treasure. The White Pearl of the Ice Dragon is one of the most valuable gems in the world," explained Panda. "This is the true quest of the wizards, not the Ice Dragon himself.

"If they could win this prize, the wizards would then no doubt go on to the Imperial City where they may choose to sell it for a great price to some nobleman. In any case, whatever their plan with the pearl, once they reach the Imperial City, having used your uncle as a guide and no doubt a lowly servant, they will surely sell him to some slave trader in the grand bazaar for a few gold coins. Such is the way wizards repay acts of kindness."

Kung looked into the deep pool, shaking his head in disbelief. It was a great burden for the simple shepherd boy.

Panda got up and came over to the boy, patting him on the head with his large soft paw.

"There, there, Kung," he said consolingly. "The Ice Dragon of this pass is one of the greatest of his race.

Perhaps the wizards will be forced back into the Enchanted Valley. Then we may hatch a plan of escape for your uncle."

Kung, whose eyes were still cast down into the pool, saw that the hundreds of brilliantly coloured fish suddenly swam into every hiding place they could find.

Panda was looking into the sky in the direction of the Dragon Pass.

"Well, in a moment we will have news of your uncle," he said. "Here comes a friend from the mountains."

THE EAGLE'S TALE

UNG LOOKED INTO THE SKY. High above the trees and bamboo tops was the biggest eagle he had ever seen. Its wide winged shadow passed over them, and as Panda waved, the bird turned and circled. Then it swept down to land on one of the low branches of the cedar tree at the edge of the pool.

The eagle stood, opening then closing its wings. The magnificent bird nodded its head to Panda as if it were bowing. Then Kung saw a strange nodding and shuffling – like some kind of silent language – passing between the bird and the Panda.

Turning for a moment, Panda saw the confused expression on Kung's face. "Apologies," he said. "I haven't introduced you. Kung the Fluteplayer, nephew of Latzu the Shepherd, this is Shang, Eagle Lord of the Dragon Pass." Kung bowed. Panda then turned to the eagle and silently sent what Kung assumed was the same message in reverse.

Panda went over to the base of the cedar tree. At its roots were many smooth, brightly coloured agates and pebbles. He stood there musing for a moment.

"Red for eagles, isn't it now?" The Eagle Lord ruffled his feathers. "No, no, quite right, Shang. It's green, isn't it?" he said, picking up a small green stone. Then Panda

walked back to Kung and gave him the green pebble.
"Here, put this in your mouth, but be careful not to
swallow it."

Obediently Kung took the smooth polished stone and
placed it in his mouth against the inside of one cheek, so
he wouldn't swallow it. Then something happened. A

voice like none Kung had ever heard before, a strange deep voice, seemed to come into his ears. "Greetings, Kung the Fluteplayer, nephew of Latzu." Kung looked around, half expecting to see someone else in the clearing. Then he looked up at the eagle.

"Yes, it is Lord Shang who speaks," said the eagle. "I'm sorry to bring you such news, my friend, but you must know the truth. Two days ago I saw your uncle and the three wizards from my eyrie on the high mountain that is the right pillar of the pass entrance, which we call the Dragon Gate. From there I watched over them in the pass until they reached the Road of the South."

"Ahem," said Panda, "excuse me, Shang, perhaps you might explain the pass to Kung."

"Ah, yes," said Shang. "The Dragon Pass is a narrow gap in the Dharka Mountains that begins at the towers of the Dragon Gate and ends at the Stone Bridge on the far side. There the foothills give way to the wide plain on which you will see the Crimson Road and the spice caravans of the south. It is in the middle of the pass, however, where the terror lies. Here you will find Emerald Lake, a cold and beautiful lake fed by a high waterfall at its northern shore. It is here that the Ice Dragon lives and all who walk the road along this north shore are in danger of being destroyed by him."

"Ice dragons," explained Panda, "do not fly or breathe flame like the fire dragons of the far north, but in the water they are as swift as fire dragons are in the air. These dragons use ice as the fire dragons use flame. Their jaws are filled with teeth like blue steel and they breathe out a frost blizzard of hail and fog and snow like a sudden winter storm. Out of this icy blizzard comes an army of phantom creatures. White wolves and white ravens who join their master in the hunt. They are hallucinations of the

dragon's breath, but they become living beasts and have a
will and desire for destruction as strong as their master's."

"Did the wizards dare to fight such a creature?" asked
Kung with disbelief.

"They did," said Shang. "When the battle began, I
thought it was a terrible thunderstorm at the head of the
lake, such was the turmoil. It shook the mountains. The
white wolves were struck down by the fiery sword of the
tallest of the wizards. The ice ravens were shot out of the
air by the archer's arrows of flame. And the spears of the
third wizard exploded, bringing up a hot black wall of
smoke and flame that kept the dragon away. Each time the

Ice Dragon launched an attack, a new spear appeared in the hand of the third wizard. The flaming arrows and the sword of the other two wizards struck at the dragon or his minions each time they attempted to breach the hot sulphurous barrier. Huge clouds of steam arose from this battle of fire and ice as they fought their way across the north shore toward the waterfall."

"Lord Shang," interrupted Kung, "was my uncle with these men during this battle?"

"Indeed he was, Kung," said Shang. "And through the wizards' wicked spells, it was he who changed the course of the battle."

"You see," explained Panda, "the wizards knew that powerful though they were, they could only defend against the Ice Dragon. They could never overcome him while he held the White Pearl, the treasure and talisman of the Ice Dragon's power."

"So it was, Kung," said Shang, "that in the din of this battle while partially under the camouflage of the high waterfall as well as the barrier of smoke and flame, the wizards bewitched your uncle and transformed him into an otter! So transformed, Latzu leaped into the arch of the falls and deep into the cold lake. There, while the Ice Dragon battled the wizards on the north shore, your uncle swam far to the south shore, the place of the towers and caves of ice. He swam into the blue fissures of the glaciers as the wizards had commanded him. Then he dived into the deepest blue grotto. There he found the magical dragon pearl which glowed like a small moon. Your uncle took the pearl in his otter mouth and swam back to the embattled wizards beneath the waterfall. Once there, he returned to his shape as a man, and the wizards snatched the pearl from him. With an evil glee they shouted and held it over their heads to show it to their enemy. When the Ice Dragon saw the pearl, he screamed in rage and fear. His ice phantoms had vanished before the possessors of the pearl, and although the dragon's great strength remained, it could not be used to crush anyone who commanded the pearl. Saddened and furious, he retreated to his ice caves in the south."

Panda turned to Shang on the limb of the tree. "I thank you, Lord Shang, for the service you give us, however sad the news. As you say, it is best to know the truth."

Shang ruffled his feathers and raised his head. "It's always an honour to serve my Lord Beishung and his friends." Then the eagle spread his wings and rose into the air, heading for the mountains in the east.

THE PANDA'S SECRET

AS SHANG the Eagle Lord flew out beyond Kung's vision, the full force of the eagle's story began to fall on Kung. He hung his head down pensively and sadly thought of his poor uncle.

Panda looked at the downcast Kung. "Do not fret too much, Kung. At least we know that your uncle has not been harmed. Come, come, we must be on our way. Get up on all fours ... or twos, in your case, and we'll be off. Things have not greatly changed. We must simply get you over the Dragon Pass and on to the Imperial City – and there you will rescue your uncle," said Panda, as if it were the most obvious conclusion in the world.

Kung nodded. Realizing he still had the green stone in his mouth, he spit it out into his hand. Rubbing it on his shirt, he placed it back under the tree with the other bright pebbles. He then hurried to catch up with Panda who had already crossed the clearing and reached a pathway into the thick bamboo and blossoming rhododendrons.

After a while, as they walked along, Kung began to think about the wizards again. He also thought about the pearl.

"Will any great harm come from the wizards' possession of the Ice Dragon's pearl?" he asked Panda.

"Well, anything that increases the wealth and power of

these wizards cannot be particularly good. However," Panda said, "the white pearls of the ice dragons, rare and valuable though they are, have no great power to harm. They are somewhat like the ice dragons themselves, which were brought into the world as a measure of balance. Do you remember when I told you how it was before the world was made by the Supreme-Being-of-the-Ninth-Heaven? The time when there was no balance or harmony? When there was just disorder and chaos?"

Kung nodded.

"Well, in that time the fiery demons of chaos forged black pearls – gems of evil – and about these were made the

terrible monsters we call the fire dragons. These fire-breathing, flying dragons with the evil black gems buried deep in their foreheads lived in the thousands in the swirling spiral of the Abyss. As you can imagine, it was difficult to build anything in the Abyss with thousands upon thousands of these beasts lumbering about the place. But eventually the Supreme-Being-of-the-Ninth-Heaven decided – on my advice, I must say – that it was best to fight fire with ice. So it was that the Supreme Being made the moon pearls, which were gems of opposite nature to the black pearls. Pearls that loved ice and light as much as the black pearls cherished fire and darkness. He dropped these white gems into the swirling Abyss. For each pearl He made an ice dragon as a guardian, and to each He gave powers opposite but equal to those of the fire dragon. Then He stood back and let nature have its way. What followed were the dragon wars. The dragons slew each other by the thousand. Finally a kind of order began to prevail in the Abyss, like the seasons of the year – spring and summer dominated by fire, autumn and winter, by ice. By the time the world was shaped, most of the dragons were gone."

The pathway twisted through another grove of asoka trees. Wading amidst the golden petals that had fallen to the earth were a score of miniature sika deer. Timid beasts though they were, they did not flee when Panda and Kung approached. They simply looked up with their large eyes, seemed to nod respectfully at Panda, then continued to graze among the leaves and petals.

"Pearls, pearls ... ah, yes," reflected Panda as they marched on. "As I was saying, the white pearls were made by the Supreme Being, and I have no fear of them being used for evil. However, had the wizards taken a black pearl, that would be a very different matter," said Panda with a shudder.

"Surely if they can rob the Ice Dragon, they can do the same with the Fire Dragon?" inquired Kung.

"You forget, Kung," said Panda. "Unlike the Ice Dragon, the Fire Dragon has the Black Pearl buried deep beneath his brow next to his evil brain. The wizards would have to slay him to win it, and this is a difficult task. But there are even greater barriers. Nearly all remaining fire dragons live far to the north in the land of Hyperborea. This is the land of the wild, flat-faced tribesmen who live on horseback. This is a land of fierce warriors even the wizards would avoid. Furthermore, Kung , no one except the Holy Men of the Forbidden Mountains knows that the black pearls exist in the brow of the fire dragons. And the Holy Men would not divulge this knowledge."

"But why is that?" asked Kung.

"I'm afraid the black pearls are beyond my power to balance and restrain. They are more ancient than even I am. They are made of a black flame of pure evil. If a black pearl were placed before my eye, I would be trapped in its evil grip and it would hold me captive. So you see, my young Kung, it would not be a happy day for me if the evil men found a black pearl," said Panda, chuckling.

"But they will not," he said firmly, and then he winked. "Because nobody knows this secret – well, *almost* nobody. There is *me*. And now, of course, there is *you*."

The Jade Ring

PANDA AND KUNG continued their journey eastward through the Enchanted Valley toward the Dragon Pass. As they went, Panda talked on, teaching Kung as much as he could about the valley – where to watch out for this swamp, what was down that trail, where the ripe pomegranates grow, where the best bamboo sprouts may be found, where there is fresh water and where there is foul. Above all, Panda showed Kung the landmarks and signs that would guide him should he ever have to make the journey alone.

As the late afternoon drew long shadows across their path, they could see the Dharka Mountains looming. Panda explained that Kung would spend one more evening in the valley. They would camp in Panda's favourite place in the forest. This was just a short distance from the Dragon Gate.

They soon reached the beautiful glade where they would spend the night. The sunlight was fading over the soft grass. At the centre of the clearing was an ancient tree. It had many hollows and fissures. Its roots reached out in all directions, and it had golden leaves and small crimson fruits. It was unlike any tree Kung had ever seen.

Panda led Kung over to a grassy knoll between the huge tree and a little fountain bubbling with clear water. The

Panda flopped onto his hindquarters, settled himself comfortably, and with a wave of the paw, invited Kung to join him.

"Well, Kung, a good day's travelling deserves the reward of a fine meal – don't you think?"

Kung could not agree more. He was very hungry. So with a flourish the Panda produced the silk napkin from his ear and handed it to Kung. And while Kung spread their picnic cloth on the grass, Panda once again began to conjure up a meal: apples, carrots, lychees, oranges, plums, bananas, a bunch of grapes, cakes of wild rice, and of course bamboo shoots. With a sleight of the paw, Panda also produced two porcelain dishes of yogurt with peaches

 and two silver cups and a silver pitcher filled with the most delicious fruit drink Kung had ever tasted. "Ah," explained Panda, "my own secret recipe – Panda Punch. Rather good, don't you think?"

And so, lifting their silver goblets to one another in a toast, they fell to the serious business of dinner.

"I beg your pardon, my Lord Beishung," said Kung after a while, "but I must seek your advice on just *how* I might rescue my uncle once I have found him. Surely I cannot overcome these evil men without some weapon. In your wisdom, do you have such a weapon I might use? I have only a little money, not enough to buy even a single dagger."

"Young man, such a question," said Panda, almost crossly. "Surely you must know I disapprove of weapons altogether – nasty, sharp, pointy things."

"But, my Lord..." began Kung.

"Do not seek to overcome by force," interrupted Panda.

"You are still a boy, Kung, and even as a man you would never have the power of these three in combat. In any case, it is not within my powers to give instruments that inflict pain. It's true, I have these big teeth, and these long claws, *and* I'm ever so strong. I mean, if I really concentrated on being that kind of creature, I could be fierce, don't you think?"

Kung looked more than a little dubious.

"I mean, I could climb up trees," continued Panda, "like any other fierce and snarling jungle beast, and leap down on travellers or marauding squirrels or lions. Like so . . . and like so . . ."

Panda was leaping about, making faces and fearful expressions. Or at least Panda thought these were meant to be dreadful. To Kung they merely looked comic. And although he could see that the Panda had sturdy teeth and claws, Kung could not imagine him in a fight. Panda was such a peaceful, cuddly creature that his act could only make Kung laugh.

"Oh, well," said Panda with a shrug. "Perhaps not. After all, where does that get you – terrorizing everybody? You just end up with no friends, and thugs and heroes come charging in to prove how brave they are by slaying the local monster. Look at the Ice Dragon. You don't get much fiercer than that. And what's that got him? A pack of wizards come out of nowhere and attack him. I often sympathize with the monsters of the world."

Panda did a few cartwheels, followed by somersaults, until he was once again sitting in front of Kung by the picnic napkin. He tossed down a couple of lychees and drained the Panda Punch from his silver cup. Folding the silk napkin – silver pitcher and cups, porcelain dishes and all – he tucked it into his right ear. Then he looked at the gloomy Kung.

"Do not abandon hope, Kung," he said. "There are other powers that will help you save your Uncle Latzu."

Panda stood on his hind legs and began searching in the hollows of the huge old tree in the clearing. It was only then that Kung noticed that the ancient tree's twisting boles, fissures and nooks were filled with treasures. There were polished stones and exotic feathers and plumes, gold ornaments and bronze figurines. The little pockets and platforms overflowed with jewels and jades and ivory images.

Panda was shuffling about, bumping over images and rummaging through the gemstones. "Hmmmm..." he mused. "Hmm de hmm de hmmm...I know it's here somewhere."

Finally, he turned about. "Ahaa!!" In the centre of

Panda's paw was a small ring of blue jade. "Well," he said, "what do you think?"

Kung looked at the ring in the Panda's paw with a little dismay. Although he didn't wish to say so, the ring looked rather inadequate for such large tasks as overcoming dragons and wizards.

"Well, it's...it's a very pretty blue," Kung said rather hesitantly.

"Very pretty blue, indeed!" said the Panda. "I'll have you know that this jade has only one equal in the world. It is cut from the one blue jade of the Emperor of China! The one blue jade that fell from the Ninth Heaven. The great blue jade ring by which the Emperor rules the Celestial Empire!"

"Still, this one is rather small, isn't it?" suggested Kung.

"Small? It's small because it just happens to be cut from the hole in the centre of the Emperor's ring!" Panda said in exasperation.

"Yes, well, I *am* honoured," said Kung politely, "but does the ring *do* anything?"

"*Do* anything? Oh, yes, of course, I was giving you the ring for some *reason*, wasn't I? Oh, now I remember," said the Panda reflectively, "there is one side effect of its being a venerable object that might prove useful to you on your journey."

"What is that?" Kung asked anxiously.

"Oh," said the Panda distantly, "it makes you invisible." And with that, he dropped the ring over his claw and vanished from sight!

The boy was astonished and delighted, for when the Panda reappeared, he handed the ring to Kung on a necklace with a clasp, and placed it around the boy's neck.

"In the end," said the Panda, "this ring may serve you better than a whole army. Use its power sparingly or others might steal it from you, and then where will you be?"

Darkness was beginning to close around them. Soon Kung could see Panda only by his white patches.

"Well," concluded Lord Beishung with a long yawn, "time to sleep. We must rise early tomorrow and get you on your way to the Dragon Pass!"

Panda and Kung curled up together in the huge treasure tree and soon they were in a deep sleep.

THE DRAGON PASS

I T WAS MID-MORNING when the Panda and Kung came to where the forests of the Enchanted Valley ended and the mountains suddenly began at the Dragon Gate. Kung had loaded his pack with fruit and rice, and the necklace with the jade ring hung around his neck. At the entrance to the gate, the Panda stopped. He looked fondly and thoughtfully at Kung.

"Well, this is where you go on alone, young man. Slip on the ring and march right through. With the ring on, the dragon won't be able to see you. Oh, I should have mentioned, he won't be able to smell you either," he said, putting a paw to his nose. "Very important with dragons. So unless you bump right into him, you will make the passage safely. Now remember, follow the winding road along the edge of the Emerald Lake. The road passes under a high waterfall and beyond through the gap between the twin peaks on the far side. Keep going until you reach the Stone Bridge. From there you will see the Spice Road, which some call the Crimson Road. On this caravan road you must travel six days to the north and then you will reach the Imperial City."

The Panda gave a little flourish with his paw, then turned about. In a moment he vanished into the bamboo forest.

Lighthearted as the Panda himself, Kung marched on, forgetting the creature who had devoured whole armies of heroes. Wearing his ring and believing his invisibility protected him from the monster, Kung skipped along, humming and whistling.

Now, *that* proved something of a mistake, for although the dragon could not *see* or *smell* Kung, he could certainly *hear* something humming and whistling down the pass. So when Kung marched along the mountain trail that wound around a bend onto a ledge that overlooked the lake with its emerald waters, the boy suddenly found himself staring into the cold blue eyes of the Ice Dragon!

The dragon was rearing a hundred feet out of the water and was poised to strike. His brilliant blue, green and purple metallic scales glinted in the cold sunlight. Icy vapours seeped out of his nostrils and from between the steel-blue teeth in his gaping crimson mouth. The monster stared at Kung, while his long claws flexed in and out in anticipation, and his serpentine body slithered and churned in the emerald waters.

The sight took Kung's breath away. He froze in his tracks but after a few moments he realized that the dragon couldn't really see him. The monster's eyes flickered with an ice-blue flame, but in fact they stared right through Kung at the empty gap in the mountain road. Slowly sliding one foot ahead, then another, Kung slipped along the roadway down the lakeshore, and away from the monster's glare.

Recovering from his fright, he took a long deep breath. Then he slid along the trail quickly but stealthily. Soon he was rewarded by the sight of the high catapulting waterfall that arched over the road. It seemed to fairly leap off the high cliff and plunge hundreds of feet into a cloud of mist and little rainbows.

At the foot of the falls, in the mist, there were dozens of islets of rock in the most fanciful shapes. Little towers here, archways there. Islets with caves and grottoes. One shaped like a lion, another like a cat, or was it a rabbit? Some even had pine trees growing on them with vines and moss.

Kung looked down the length of the lake where his uncle had searched for the dragon's grotto. Far down the south end of the lake stood huge glacial walls and towers of ice etched with turquoise fissures and caverns. It was below those towers of ice that his uncle had dived to find the dragon's grotto and the great pearl.

Just then there came a furious stomping about down at the dragon side of the lake, and the road shook. A blizzard of hail, icy fog and snow filled the air about the slithering beast. Along with the roaring and thundering of the dragon himself, the air was filled with the howling of wolves and the croaking of ravens. The Ice Dragon had grown impatient waiting for his prey, and sent his ice creatures to confront the intruder.

Most of the ice wolves and ice ravens went down the trail toward the Dragon Gate, but a few flew and loped along the road in Kung's direction, peering and sniffing to no avail. Kung leapt to one side of the trail and up on a rock to avoid them running into him. Six of the ice wolves galloped along the road right past Kung without noticing a thing. They were fierce creatures with green eyes and blue teeth and crimson tongues. As they went along, they were constantly snapping and biting at the air and at each other.

Once they passed, Kung climbed down on the path again and quickly moved along under the great roaring falls and onto the twisting road. He believed he was now clear, but as he was rounding a bend and took a last look at the distant form of the dragon, he collided with an ice wolf!

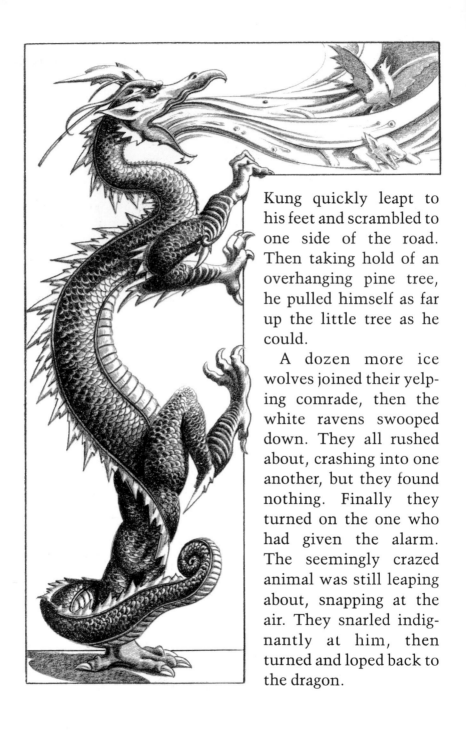

Kung quickly leapt to his feet and scrambled to one side of the road. Then taking hold of an overhanging pine tree, he pulled himself as far up the little tree as he could.

A dozen more ice wolves joined their yelping comrade, then the white ravens swooped down. They all rushed about, crashing into one another, but they found nothing. Finally they turned on the one who had given the alarm. The seemingly crazed animal was still leaping about, snapping at the air. They snarled indignantly at him, then turned and loped back to the dragon.

The offended wolf remained for a while longer, listening intently but hearing nothing. Then he snorted in disgust and trotted away.

Eventually Kung climbed down the pine tree and leapt onto the path again, then ran off in the direction of the Twin Peaks. He did not look back until he had reached the gap in the mountains at the far side of the lake. As he was putting the ring back on his necklace chain, he heard a high and distant call. He looked far above the brilliant waters of the lake and saw an eagle circling. It was Shang. Kung waved and the eagle tipped his wings in salute, then arched back and away toward the Enchanted Valley. The Master Panda would soon learn of Kung's success.

——— N·I·N·E ———

The Caravan Road

L ATE THE FOLLOWING DAY Kung crossed a small stone
bridge and set eyes on the imperial Spice Road. The
magnificent road stretched from as far as Kung
could see in the south to as far as he could see in the north.
It was paved with perfectly cut white stones, except for

the large curbstones which were imperial red.

More amazing than the road were those who travelled upon it. Never had Kung seen so many strange people and exotic animals. There were caravan trains of camels loaded with spice, great carts pulled by oxen, painted and carved circus caravans pulled by powerful horses. There were monks and monkeys, elephants and emirs, jewelled merchants and maidens. There were troupes of dancing girls. There was one cart pulled by two tigers. There were tiny men with huge dancing bears.

The spectacle seemed endless, but Kung eventually abandoned his seat on the bridge wall and hurried to join in this procession of life.

When Kung at last placed his foot on the imperial road, a parade of soldiers armed with long curved swords and dressed in leopard skins had just passed. Coming toward him was a troupe of jugglers, acrobats, musicians and actors. They had three caravans towed by black horses, and followed by an elephant and a beautiful, prancing white Unicorn being led on a silk rope by a young boy.

As Kung stood on the crimson curb of the road, watching them pass, many of the troupe greeted him cheerfully or waved. Kung returned their greetings with a polite bow or a smile.

When the boy with the Unicorn came alongside Kung, he stopped before him. The boy was about Kung's age. He wore no shirt or shoes but had a scarlet sash tied around the waist of his white cotton trousers. A red headband was wrapped around his long black hair.

But Kung could not remove his eyes from the Unicorn.

"Beautiful, isn't he?" said the boy.

Kung was awestruck and simply nodded.

"Where are you going?" asked the boy.

"To the Imperial City," Kung said at last.

"Of course. Everyone who takes this road does. Would you like to join us?"

And along Kung went with his new companion. He learned about the lands to the south from whence came elephants, gemstones, jungle beasts and unicorns. But, above all, the southern realms were known for their treasury of spices. Rani, for such was this boy's name, was himself from the Spice Islands beyond Siam.

When Rani was only five years old he was walking in the forest near his home when he heard the sound of an animal thrashing about desperately. He followed the sound and found that a young Unicorn had fallen into a tiger trap and hurt its leg. Rani and his father and brother managed to lift the poor animal out of the pit, but the injury was so severe that Rani's father feared the Unicorn would not survive.

Young Rani refused to give up on the animal. He nursed it night and day for many months until it was restored to health. The bond that had grown between Rani and the Unicorn was so strong that when it was well enough, it chose to stay with Rani rather than return to the forest.

Rani's family was poor, so when he was ten he and the Unicorn joined a theatre troupe so he might earn money for his family. This had been Rani's life since then, and he enjoyed it beyond measure.

"This year," Rani said excitedly to Kung, "we have been summoned to the Imperial Court to entertain the Emperor himself!"

Kung thought that Rani's life of travelling and performing with the Unicorn was so much more exciting than his own in Sung Wu.

For two days he travelled with the theatre troupe and came to know many of the performers: the jugglers, the strongmen, the elephant and his trainer, and a few dancers and actors. During those two days Kung and Rani became fast friends. Kung told Rani of his search for his kidnapped uncle and Rani swore to help him.

On the third night, Kung was sitting by the fire with Rani and a few other friends, while the Unicorn grazed behind them. The troupe's musicians suddenly formed a procession from their nearby fire and came over to Kung and Rani, playing their mandolins and lutes and chimes and gongs and drums as they paraded in their gay costumes. One of the musicians noticed that Kung had a flute. "Show us what kind of music is played in the realm of Sung Wu!"

Kung was rather shy, but finally he took out his bamboo flute and began to play.

Kung's melody lulled the listeners, then it entranced them. It seemed to be a music that came out of their lives like the happiest memories and dreams of childhood. They would not let him stop. A beautiful girl from Siam with gold coins in her hair and rings on her fingers began to dance as if she were on the waves of the sea. "Again!" they called out. And as Kung played on, something brushed against his shoulder, and he turned to see the Unicorn.

To everyone's amazement, the creature stood up on its hind legs, threw back its head and began to dance. It danced around the Fluteplayer, turning and turning on its hind legs. Seeing the Unicorn's delight in his music, Kung stood up too and began to dance. Kung and the Unicorn danced around the campfire while the audience clapped to the rhythm of the flute and the beating of the hooves.

"You must remain with us," said Rani. "Your three copper coins will not be enough to keep you in the Imperial City for a day. We'll stay in the Inn of the Lute and if you will perform with me and my Unicorn for just one night in the Imperial Court, you will be rewarded with enough gold coins to buy your uncle's freedom."

Kung sat for a moment, fingering his flute, then he turned brightly to Rani. "Thank you, my friend. I must not refuse an opportunity that fortune has placed before me."

Rani was delighted. "Just think," he said, "I shall ride a dancing Unicorn and you shall play your flute before the Emperor! And together we shall rescue your uncle."

THE IMPERIAL CITY

THE IMPERIAL CITY! Not even in Kung's most extravagant dreams had he imagined the city was as grand as it truly was. Since the soldiers allowed them to pass over the White Bridge and through the Ivory Gate at dawn, they had been travelling through the imperial game parks that encircled the city. The road passed through forests, green swards and little lakes with decorative fountains. Lords and ladies walked or rode in hunting costume or sat in bright pavilions as others contested with bows or javelins. Here and there golden elk drank from woodland streams or herds of milk-white deer grazed in open fields.

It took the troupe half a day to travel the straight road through the royal reserve where none hunted save at the Emperor's pleasure. It was noon when they came at last to the walls of the city. From afar Kung had thought they were coming onto a mountain, so vast were the city's parapets and defences. It would take an army of dragons to breach such walls, Kung thought, even if they were all as fierce as the Ice Dragon of Dharka. When at last the massive cedar and iron gate was opened, a city of millions rose before Kung's eyes: buildings and towers and temples and pagodas greater than any Kung could have imagined beneath the Ninth Heaven.

The city was filled with markets and bazaars. Thousands thronged the streets, but from each of the gates in the four directions ran the broad straight roads that led to still another great wall. This was a citadel surmounted by towers and spires. Above all stood the imperial palace. It reached up into the sky, leaving all below in the shadow of its crimson and gold rooftops and streaming silk banners.

It was nearly evening by the time the troupe had worked its way through the thronging streets to the destination of their inn near the palace wall. This was the Inn of the Lute. It was a large but modest inn favoured by theatre troupes, musicians and other performers. This was partly because it provided stables for beasts and had a large courtyard in which they might practise and play, but mostly its popularity was due to the genial owner who was once an actor himself.

The innkeeper greeted them warmly. He was a large, round Mongolian with long, drooping moustaches, dressed in a red tunic and leather apron. He had the deep voice and hearty laugh of an old thespian. He called for his servants to stable the animals and led the caravans behind the inn. Then he brought one and all into the big dining room and set them down at the table. His staff scurried about for drink and food.

Laughter and music mingled with the food and talk. Kung and Rani made the most of the meal, for like the others, they were truly hungry. There was a fine, filling soup to start, then large steaming plates of fish and fowl and meat. There were heaping bowls of noodles and rice, and plates with mushrooms and a dozen vegetables in as many different spicy sauces. As soon as one dish was emptied, another took its place.

The innkeeper entertained them for many hours, celebrating their good fortune at having been chosen to perform in the Emperor's court. It was the highest point in any performer's career.

The next day Kung and most of the troupe were in the courtyard preparing for the evening's event. The Emperor would entertain a thousand lords and ladies in each of his twelve halls. Each hall would have three troupes of entertainers. Kung's troupe had been among the most honoured, for they were to perform in the twelfth hall, before the Emperor himself and specially chosen lords and ladies.

Kung was brushing the Unicorn's smooth coat and Rani was polishing his ivory horn when Sari, the Siamese girl who danced to Kung's music, came to them, smiling brightly. With her came the innkeeper, who greeted them in his hearty manner. Rani had told Sari of Kung's wish to find his uncle.

"It may take a little time, my boy," said the innkeeper, "but we'll not rest until we've looked in every one of the thousand markets. And tonight in the Emperor's court you will earn the gold to buy your uncle's freedom." With a smile and a slap of reassurance on Kung's back, the inn-keeper was off about his business, and Kung and Rani went on with their grooming.

From time to time courtiers and ladies would wander into the courtyard of the inn to get a preview of the entertainers for the evening. They would often come and watch for a while, comment or joke to one another, then move on. Among such a group of nobles Kung became aware of a dark pair of eyes focussed intently on him. When he looked up to them he was amazed to find they belonged to the most beautiful girl he had ever seen. She wore robes of intricately embroidered yellow silk. She had a pale, beautiful oval face, large black eyes with high eyebrows and jet hair. She was obviously a lady of the high court, although she was only Kung's age.

Startled at being caught staring at Kung, the girl raised her ivory fan over her face. Then she turned to the other court ladies as they admired the various performers.

As the group moved around the fringe of the courtyard, the girl in the yellow silk robe glanced over her fan again. When at last the group was turning to leave, the girl lowered her fan. She looked back at Kung and gave the boy a small smile. Then she turned and went out the gate.

Kung continued to stare at the courtyard gate after the girl had vanished. Then Rani noticed that he was the only one working on the Unicorn's harness, so he gave Kung a nudge. "What's the matter? Asleep on your feet?"

Kung smiled sheepishly. As he prepared himself and the Unicorn for the evening, the face of the beautiful girl floated in his thoughts like a little moon. She might as well be the moon, he thought sadly, I am as likely to speak to her as I am to speak to the moon.

The Emperor

N THE LATE AFTERNOON Kung and Rani stood with the whole troupe before the great bronze doors in the citadel walls. The Unicorn gently nuzzled them as a disdainful gatekeeper inspected the document that commanded them to perform before the court.

Kung and Rani were dressed identically in white tunics and trousers with red headbands and sashes. Kung listened to the fluttering of the silk banners on the high wall and noticed the rose tint of the late sun as it glinted on the armour of the guardsmen that stood on either side of the gatekeeper.

At last a guardsman guided Kung and the troupe through the gate and the ornamental gardens to the palace itself.

The Emperor's palace with its crimson and gold rooftops and tall pillars was the largest and most magnificent building in all the world. It was made of white marble and painted and gilded with bird, beast and flower. The doors were set with jades and the chambers fitted with bronze vessels and ebony furniture.

Kung and Rani, along with all the others in the troupe, were stunned at the grandeur about them. In silence they were led to a courtyard within the palace and each taken by a servant and shown his luxurious bed chamber. Each room was fitted with tapestries and carpets and a soft bed with silk sheets.

When the time came Kung, Rani and the others were summoned into a waiting room just off the big feasting hall. About them were magicians and jugglers, clowns and acrobats, swordsmen and strongmen. Near Kung was a tiger tamer talking sternly to his three ferocious beasts. The tigers sat politely in front of him and lapped milk from their saucers. A snake charmer on a bench opposite Rani was trying to coil up his three-headed cobra into a woven basket. All around, performers made their last-minute preparations.

Kung sat quietly and held his flute in his hands, calming himself by running his fingers up and down the instrument. Rani had gone to the hall entrance and peered through the crack in the partially opened doors. After a short while he called Kung to join him.

Peeking through the crack, Kung and Rani watched as a fire-breathing swordsman and two archers performed with a magician who caused golden cups to fly about the hall. From time to time a cup would fly up to a lord or lady, and they would pluck it from the air and drink.

The hall was huge. Long tapestries hung from gilded walls and tall pillars were surmounted by carved dragons with their tails wound around the columns and their heads supporting the roof. Their wide wings spread like buttresses to the high ceiling. Lords, ladies, generals and statesmen were seated around the central court where the entertainers performed. The ebony tables were heaped with every kind of food that the world offered. The guests drank from cups and chalices of silver and gold; they ate from plates and bowls of finest porcelain and lacquerwork. And wandering all about the feasting guests were guardsmen and messengers, serving maids and boys, jugglers and clowns, soothsayers and harp players.

At the far end of the hall was a raised platform and a high table. Here the Emperor sat on a gold throne with a beautiful maiden at his side, and his twelve chief governors about him. The Emperor was a large, elderly man with rather fierce moustaches. He wore a white silk tunic under his black ceremonial robe embroidered with gold thread and jewels in the form of fighting dragons. Resting on his breast, suspended on a broad silk ribbon, was a blue jade ring: the Sky Ring, of which Panda had spoken.

There was someone else at the high table, however, who drew Kung's attention far more intently than even the Emperor. Much to his astonishment, he recognized the beautiful girl who sat by the Emperor's side. It was the same girl who had so enchanted him in the courtyard that very afternoon! Kung soon learned that she was none other than the Princess Li Su, the Emperor's only child.

As Rani and the Unicorn galloped into the court, there came immediate applause. The Unicorn pranced about the room while Rani first rode sitting, then standing, then doing a handstand and finally a headstand before the lords and ladies. The Unicorn galloped to the sound of drums and lutes, then suddenly the music stopped. Sari, the dancer, stood on one side holding the Unicorn's reins; Rani dismounted and stood on the other side. The Unicorn went down on one knee, bowing deeply to the Emperor, its nose and horn touching the flagstones.

As all looked on, there came the sound of a flute, low at first, gentle and beautiful. It seemed to fill the vast hall with a strange ethereal music. But where was the flute-player? Suddenly, by some magical act, he appeared in the centre of the court between the Unicorn and the Emperor. There he joined the Unicorn in a bow of respect as he

continued to play. It was Kung of course. He used his jade ring for what the court took to be a conjurer's trick. He raised his head to look up to the Emperor—and to the Princess, who looked back with a shy smile of recognition. Then he turned to the Unicorn, and the beautiful beast rose up on its hind legs, tossed back its head and began to dance on two legs.

The acrobats tumbled and juggled in a wide circle about them. Kung's flute sang out, the Unicorn's hooves rang on the marble floor. The lords, ladies and the Emperor himself became entranced with both sight and sound. They began to beat the floor and tables with the rhythms of the Unicorn's dance, just as the others on the Crimson Road had done that first night by the fire.

Joyfully, Rani and Sari joined in with an acrobatic dance, the Unicorn turning and dancing between them as Kung played.

When the performance ended at last, there were cheers and calls of praise. From the high table even the Emperor smiled and raised his cup. At his side the Princess Li Su smiled warmly and applauded with the rest of the court. And the fluteplayer and the Unicorn were rewarded with a purse of gold coins.

THE PRINCESS

AS KUNG LAY on the silk sheets in the Emperor's court, he thought of his uncle, who was no doubt lying in some foul dungeon. He could not sleep. He began thinking of what he might do to find his uncle and buy his freedom with his newly earned gold. But the city was so vast and there were many markets where slaves were bought and sold.

Kung climbed out of bed and went into the courtyard gardens. The night was warm, but the light of the nearly full moon was like a white frost on the pavement. Kung sat on a stone bench and began to play his flute. He played, as he had so often done in Sung Wu, to the moon.

After he had played softly for some time, Kung felt somewhat consoled. Then a small voice called out from the dark: "Thank you, Fluteplayer, that was beautiful."

Kung could see no one in the shadowy courtyard. Then he looked up at the gallery and beheld the lovely white face of the princess in the silk robe.

"My Princess!" said a startled Kung, going down on his knees and bowing deeply.

"Rise, Fluteplayer, you need not bow so low to me in such a private place," said the Princess Li Su, rather amused by Kung's awe.

But Kung did not rise. Remaining bowed, he said, "But, my Princess, surely I am not worthy to speak with you.

Surely the Emperor would not permit me such a privilege."

"In my judgement, you are worthy enough to speak to any in the realm, my Fluteplayer," said the Princess. "And my father has other concerns these days which demand higher priority than who speaks to his daughter. He leaves that discretion to me." The Princess pouted. "However, it is I who must beg your pardon, for I have been the intruder. So if you wish to be left to the peace of your thoughts and your music, I will now leave." And she turned from the balcony railing.

"Oh, no, my Princess," said Kung, leaping up. "I meant no such thing. There is nothing more I could wish for than to have your company!" Kung was astonished at his boldness, but the words seemed to come of their own accord.

The Princess turned back to Kung. She smiled and placed her hands on the railing of the balcony. "Well, now you have my company."

Kung was at a loss as to what to say to the Princess.

"Before I spoke, while you were playing your flute, what were you thinking?" asked Li Su. "It was such a gentle but sad tune."

"I was thinking," said Kung, taking a breath, "of my uncle, who is called Latzu the Shepherd. You see, I have come to the Imperial City to find him, for he was kidnapped in Sung Wu and has been brought here to be bartered in the slave markets. And I fear he will be taken to some far province before I can find him."

"This is a terrible thing," said the Princess after a thoughtful pause, "but I believe I can help you find your uncle. At first light tomorrow I will have guardsmen search each of the slave markets. Then you may go and purchase your uncle's release with your gold coins."

"Oh, my Princess!" said Kung, completely overwhelmed. "I don't know how I can thank you. The blessings of the Nine Heavens upon you and your ancestors."

"There is no need, Fluteplayer. You are a loyal subject who has been wronged. It is the duty of those who rule to be just and generous. Had my father heard your case, he would have done what little I have offered, and even more. Or, at least, he would have in earlier days," she said a little sadly, "before the death of my mother, the Empress."

"It is sad to lose a parent," said Kung sympathetically. "I was very young when my parents were swept away in a pestilence. That is why my Uncle Latzu is so dear to me. He is all I have."

"In a way, I feel I too have lost both my parents," said Princess Li Su. "My father suffers on, and in his grief he is only half alive. I miss the father I once had. Since my mother's death, his concerns with the empire have faded. And all he ever seems to think of is the Imperial Collection."

"The collection?" asked Kung.

"When my father lost his Empress, he believed there was no use in pursuing happiness in this life. Instead, he decided he would have the immortality of fame. One day I found him in the Imperial Library with all the old books and manuscripts scattered about him. There was *The Bamboo Book*, *The Book of the Sages*, *The Book of Histories*, *The Silk Book of the Masters*, *The Book of Changes* and many others. But when he glanced up at me, his face had a look of despair.

"'What's the use?' he said. 'All the great deeds have been done. The roads have been built, the lands dammed and cultivated, the great philosophies written.'

"He knew he could not rebuild Emperor Chin's Great Wall. He knew he would never live as long as the Emperor Shen Nung, the Ancient One. He knew he could never be wise as the emperor whom we call the Divine Yao. He complained that Huang Tu, the Yellow Emperor, had once conquered all the people of the world, and the Great Yu managed to create more wealth than anyone under the Nine Heavens might even imagine. 'What is there left to do?' he lamented over and over.

"It was shortly after that day in the library that he came on the idea of his collection. He had discovered a book made by scholarly monks in ancient times. It was called *The Book of Magical Beasts*. After reading this natural history of all the world's distant and exotic creatures, he decided what his mission in life was to be. He would collect from all parts of the world the most wonderful and magical of animals. His collection would be the wonder of the world. And that is what he has done. However, he pursues this project with such intensity that I fear he neglects all other matters of state."

Kung looked at the sad face of the Princess. Above all, he wished to help and comfort her. "Oh, my Princess, I am only a humble servant, but any deed you wish to ask of me, I will attempt with all my heart and soul."

The Princess looked down on Kung. "By listening to my problems with a sympathetic ear, you have made me feel less alone. There is something I sense in your music and your voice that is noble and uplifting. If only there were a man such as you in the royal court, the empire would be greatly served."

The Princess turned to leave. "Tomorrow is the Festival of the Moon. Come to the temple grounds early and see my father's grand collection. By then I should also have word of your uncle."

As the Princess disappeared, Kung lifted his flute and played the sweetest lullaby he knew.

THE EMPEROR'S COLLECTION

KUNG AWOKE FEELING refreshed and excited. He leapt out of bed, then he went and woke Rani in the next chamber. The two boys laughed and joked about their success before the Emperor, and after a while Kung spoke to Rani of his late-night meeting with the Princess and how she had promised to help him find his uncle.

Soon they went with the rest of the troupe to a lavish morning meal in a large breakfast room in their quarter of the palace. Then, on being extended once again the thanks and pleasure of

the Emperor, they all departed from the palace to the troupe's quarters at the Inn of the Lute. Here the troupe would happily remain for a time and spend their newly earned gold in the shops and markets of the city.

Kung, of course, had more urgent business. By mid-morning he and Rani were making their way toward the Temple of the Moon in the west sector of the city.

In a short time they came to the walled sanctuary that encircled the temple. It was in this large and beautiful garden that the Emperor chose to place his collection of magical beasts. This sanctuary of the moon seemed an appropriate place for the collection because, as the devout knew, the goddess of the moon was the guardian of all creatures of the wild. So in the wide gardens among the tall cypresses, the monkey puzzle and sacred ginkgo trees, there were the ornate and beautiful cages and enclosures of the most exotic creatures in the world.

Kung and Rani walked among the crowds who had come to the Festival of the Moon and who wandered about, gazing at the Emperor's amazing collection.

The first cage that Kung and Rani came to contained a

Phoenix. The fabulous bird was standing unhurt and totally unconcerned in the midst of a roaring fire. The next cage contained two beasts with human parts to them. One, a Centaur, was half man and half horse. The other, a Minotaur, half bull and half man. Then there was the nine-headed serpent, the Hydra; and in the next cage, the two-headed, six-legged Blue Tiger of Annam. In a silver cage by a cypress tree there lounged a Sphinx, a winged lion with the beautiful face and breasts of a woman.

There was a huge aquarium tank with a massive Kraken slithering its giant tentacles about, and another tank with a Mermaid and a Merman. In a third tank—much to Rani's delight—they saw a Sea Unicorn.

There were many other enclosures with all manner of creatures: crystal stags, fanged deer, horned rabbits. There was a Griffon and a Flying Horse—and even a creature that was part of each, called a Hippogriff.

Most spectacular of all, however, were the dragons. There were both sorts: fire and ice. Being natural enemies, they were kept at opposite ends of the gardens.

As Kung wandered among the enclosures, he saw that

Rani had gone off to see a Blue Unicorn in an ivory cage and seemed deep in conversation with two of the keepers. Both were very short and stocky men dressed in silk jackets embroidered with the emblem of the imperial service. One carried a bucket and the other a shovel and both had beards and wore strange caps.

"...and does the Emperor only hire gnomes like yourselves as keepers here?" Rani was asking the curious little men as Kung approached.

"Oh, no, not at all," one said, smiling. "There are many kinds of folk who are keepers here, even a few giants. But the Emperor has found that gnomes and dwarfs seem to get along with certain beasts better than the big folk."

"Except for the Gorgon!" snorted the other, rather grumpy keeper. "Everyone who looks at it turns into stone. And the Emperor insists that gnomes do *all* the work around this beast."

"Well, that's a sore point," shrugged the first gnome, "but what is there to say? It's not that the Emperor wants us to turn to stone. But if there is an accident, the Emperor seems to think we make far more decorative garden sculpture than ordinary keepers."

At that moment the silver gong of the Temple of the Moon was being struck. The festival was to begin. So Kung and Rani bid the gnomes farewell and joined the stream of spectators that flowed onto the lawns before the Temple of the Moon.

THE FESTIVAL OF THE MOON

THE EMPEROR was seated on his peacock throne. Beside him on a smaller throne was his daughter, the Princess Li Su. On his other side stood the tall, white-robed High Priestess of the Moon. She wore two silver serpent bracelets wrapped around her arms and a silver crescent about her neck.

All were on the great balcony of the pillared Temple of the Moon. Standing before the temple were a hundred handmaidens in white silk and a hundred guardsmen in silver armour.

Kung and Rani stood on the lawns before the temple with the thousands who had gathered for the opening of the festival.

As the Emperor rose he took the jade ring from his neck and raised it high over his head. All before him bowed to this sign of office. Lowering the ring, he began the traditional address of the Festival of the Moon. It was an ancient poem dedicated to the moon's beauty and its power over the fate of the people and the empire.

Then began the proclamations, the pardons, the granting of petitions, the dividing of land, the awarding of honours. All was attended with pomp and ceremony—sometimes the burning of paper sacrifices on the altar or the gift of images in gold or jade.

Finally, as the ceremonies seemed to be nearing the end, the Emperor sat in silence for a time, and a quiet descended about the temple. Then he spoke up in a deeply thoughtful way.

"Know ye all that emperors, as all men, desire the immortality of fame. In this I am no different from any other who has come to rule his people. Here, in these gardens, you see the evidence of my bid for immortality." With a broad gesture the Emperor swept his arms out over the gardens where the sun glinted on the gilded cages and the birds and beasts in his spectacular collection sang or bellowed.

"But my task is not yet achieved. My collection is not complete. I have consulted the oracles and the seers, and my course of action is clear. I now announce, my subjects, that my daughter is to wed."

A great cheer arose from the throng. There was to be a royal wedding! The people leapt up in celebration of the coming event.

"Be still, my people," the Emperor commanded, holding up his hand. "To fulfil her destiny, my daughter is to wed the one who brings to the Imperial Court the rarest and most magical of all creatures: the ancient one called Lord Beishung, the Panda!"

It seemed to Kung that everyone gasped in disbelief. But the Emperor spoke again.

"Do not take this to be some whim of an old man. Only with the capture of this rarest of beasts will my collection be completed—and my fame assured. I have consulted the oracles on this matter. The Great Panda still lives in a secret place in the realm of the empire, though without success I have searched many years for him. There is one, the oracles say, who will find him and bring him to my court, and to this man will go the hand of my daughter. Such is my proclamation! Let it be so. And so too let the ceremonies end and the Festival of the Moon begin."

And with that, the silver gong was struck and the silver trumpets were blown. The people cheered and the Emperor turned from them and walked into the inner sanctuaries of the temple. And the Princess Li Su bowed her head and followed.

As the crowds dispersed and moved again through the gardens, Kung and Rani stayed on.

"What a strange way to marry off a daughter—even for an emperor," said the puzzled Rani.

"Yes," Kung agreed thoughtfully as he moved toward the entrance of the temple.

"I am Kung the Fluteplayer of Sung Wu," he said to the guardsman. "The Princess Li Su has requested I report to the temple after the opening ceremonies of the festival."

The guardsman looked down on him. Removing his helmet, he placed it under his arm. "Yes, you are expected," he said. "You will follow me." He then turned on his heel and marched through the entranceway.

The guardsman brought Kung and Rani into a waiting room opening onto a small garden within the temple. In a short time there was the whispering of silk on stone and in the doorway there appeared the Princess Li Su and two ladies-in-waiting.

Kung and Rani bowed deeply to the Princess, but she bid them rise and smiled. However, Kung could see that tears had fallen down the cheeks of that lovely face. He knew then that she must be deeply unhappy with her father's announcement.

"My master Fluteplayer and his friend the Unicorn

Rider are most welcome company," she said. "But for you, Fluteplayer, I have news of your uncle. Come and walk with me here in the garden and I will tell you of it—if your friend doesn't mind? My ladies will attend him as we talk."

Rani bowed again in assent, and Kung and the Princess walked out into the garden.

"My friend, your Uncle Latzu is, as you guessed, in the slave traders' markets," said the Princess. "And though weak from hunger and exhaustion, he is not greatly harmed."

"Oh, my Princess, I cannot thank you enough," exclaimed Kung, much relieved. "Where may I find him then?"

"He is in the Market of the Iron Scales," said the Princess. "I will have one of my servants take you to him within the hour."

Kung was so delighted that the Princess had to smile. But with that smile Kung remembered her troubles.

"My Princess, there is no way I can repay your kindness except with my word of sincere thanks. I can see it is a troublesome time for you as well."

At these words the Princess turned her face away. "Well," she said at last, "it gives me some pleasure in a time of personal sadness to help resolve the misfortunes of others. Although I must not speak of my father's decision as a misfortune. Perhaps it is great wisdom that is hidden from me. A princess must obey the will of the emperor and be a model for her subjects."

After a long pause Kung spoke quietly. "Perhaps, my Princess, I may be of some comfort to you. I have recently come upon a source of Panda lore that I'm sure is accurate. I believe your father has set your suitors an impossible task. Although it seems that the Master Panda is still within the realm of the empire, it is not possible for any man to capture him. Perhaps your father in his wisdom has set this impossible task to delay the day of parting with his only daughter."

The Princess listened carefully to Kung's words. "Perhaps I misjudge my father. Perhaps his plan is as you say, or another of which neither of us has thought. But I can see that you know something that others do not. So perhaps, after all, you will be my champion and protector. Yes, I take comfort from your words," said the Princess, deeply touched by Kung's concern.

As a servant led Kung away to find his uncle, he bowed again to the Princess Li Su. When he raised his head, their eyes met for a tender moment. It seemed that an impossible wish and secret pledge remained there in the garden and in their hearts.

THE SLAVE MARKET

OR NEARLY AN HOUR the Princess' servant led Kung and Rani through the maze of markets in the Imperial City. Through vegetable and fruit markets, clothing markets, rug bazaars and markets selling translucent porcelain, bright tiles and glazed pots. Then there were the workshops of the iron mongers, leather workers and glass blowers, and after these the shops of the craftsmen who worked in silver and gold, and still more shops where men bartered for crystals and gems.

Finally the servant brought them into one of the many slave markets, and at last the one called the Market of the Iron Scales. Here wealthy, lavishly dressed men gathered before the auction platforms lining the streets. On the platforms were forlorn-looking men and women and sometimes entire families chained together and offered up for sale.

After passing nearly a dozen auction blocks, the servants stopped before one. It was like any of the others: a raised wooden platform in front of a grey stone building that contained the holding cells of the slaves. There were iron bars on the windows and an iron grate doorway. Two slavers with swords in their belts stood talking by the doorway, while the third was auctioning off two young girls.

The Princess' servant turned to Kung and pointed to the smaller of the two men, a brown-skinned Simian with a shaved head and a black patch over one eye.

"That is the man to speak to, Master Kung. The imperial guardsmen spoke to him this morning. They believe your uncle is in his charge. The guardsmen ordered the slaver to sell the old man to no one save you."

Kung could see that the Simian slaver and his partner were looking toward them. They had recognized the livery of the imperial servant. The servant bowed to the slavers in acknowledgement, then bowed to Kung and Rani, and took his leave.

The one-eyed man walked toward them. "You'd be the ones come about the old man, arc you?" His crooked smile and scarred face added to the menace in the voice.

Kung spoke up firmly. "Yes, we've come for the man called Latzu from the land of Sung Wu."

"Just the right age yourselves for the best prices on the auction block, aren't you? I'd find buyers for you right away," he said, pinching the flesh on Kung's arm.

In an instant Rani was at Kung's side, sweeping away the slaver's arm with one hand. With his other hand on the dagger handle in his sash, he stood before the man with a deadly and menacing look on his face.

Both the slaver and Kung were startled by Rani's sudden ferocity. The slaver stepped back a pace. Then he shrugged and smiled his crooked smile.

"Hot little gypsy, aren't we? Cool down, my lad, do you think I would dare harm one who comes from the Imperial Court? It would be a short life for me."

With that, the slaver turned and walked toward the iron door. Kung and Rani followed him as he sorted out the keys on an iron ring. Finding the key, he opened the creaking door and the three walked down the dark and damp gallery which was lined on either side with straw-strewn cells. At the far end of the gallery, the Simian pointed through the iron bars of the last cell. There was an old man with white hair dressed only in a loincloth and the tatters of a cotton shirt lying on a pile of straw.

"Uncle Latzu!" Kung cried. "Uncle Latzu, it's me, Kung."

The old man looked up slowly, and upon seeing Kung, he smiled.

"Ah, my boy, what good fortune. I have long prayed to see you again, though I thought therc was no hope. So many obstacles between Sung Wu and the Imperial City, yet by some miracle you have reached me. My prayers have been answered."

But Latzu was too weak to stand up and greet Kung, and so remained lying on his straw mattress.

Kung looked at the Simian who stood by the cell door, tapping the key in his hand. There was a dead look in the man's face. No pity or compassion touched the soul of this merchant of human flesh.

"Will you not open the door?" said Kung, more as a command than a question.

"First the payment, my lad. Five gold pieces for the old man," he said flatly.

Kung quickly took the coins from his purse and counted them into the slaver's open hand.

"No bargaining?" asked the slaver, a little surprised. "Well, well, in that case I should have asked for more," he said with a dry laugh. Then he turned the key and opened the door.

Kung went into the cell and going down on his knees embraced Latzu on the straw. Tears of joy were in the eyes of both, for though Latzu was not well, Kung could see it was not a deadly illness. What had seemed an impossible task such a short time ago in the far-off land of Sung Wu had now been accomplished. Kung had rescued his beloved uncle.

THE BLACK PEARL

URING THE NEXT FEW DAYS Kung, with the help of Sari the dancing girl, managed to cure Latzu of his fever and illness.

As he recovered he told Kung his tale of woe. "They were mighty wizards indeed," said Latzu. "I'm ashamed I aided them in their evil quest, but I was powerless against their spells."

"And in the end," said Sari, "they discarded you for a few gold coins. What villains!"

After a time Latzu told Kung how the wizards had first discovered the Dragon Pass and the Sleeping Bamboo. One night Latzu had overheard them boasting of their evil deeds.

"Evidently, they stormed one of the monastery fortresses of the Forbidden Mountains and looted it," he said. "Among their discoveries was a secret book kept by one of the Holy Men. In this book they read about the special treasure of the Ice Dragon of Dharka and of the secret road—and even of my dear friend, the Master Panda!"

"Did they speak of the Fire Dragon's treasure?" Kung ventured to ask.

"Yes," said Latzu, amazed at his nephew's question. "And some nonsense about giving Panda a shock. And about a black gem or pearl."

Kung's blood ran cold at the mention of the Black Pearl, but not wishing to alarm his uncle, he said nothing.

Soon Sari returned with hot lentil soup for Uncle Latzu, and Kung used this moment to slip away. There was much he had to do. He had terrible forebodings.

As he walked out of the Inn of the Lute he met Rani in the street. He was just returning to the inn with one of the gnomes whom the two boys had met in the Emperor's gardens. Rani and the gnomes had become friends in the past few days and he often talked to them about the animals in their care.

On seeing the gnome, Kung asked if anything unusual had been happening among the beasts in the Emperor's Collection.

The gnome looked at Kung with surprise. "Have you not heard of the vandalism in the gardens?"

Kung had been at his uncle's side these last few days and had only been concerned with Latzu's recovery.

"On the second night after the festival," the gnome reported, "terrible powers were loose in the city. That night a thunderstorm overcame the imperial guardsmen. It was no ordinary storm, but a sorcerer's storm which blinded and confused them. At the cage of a captive fire dragon there was a fierce battle. Finally the cage was burst open and the fire dragon slain. Its head had been split wide open. None could make any sense of it. Why was the great beast mutilated?"

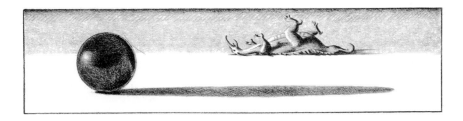

Kung could have guessed the evil plan of the wizards, even if Latzu had not told him of the stolen book from the Forbidden Mountains. His worst fears were realized and a shudder ran through his body.

"Why do you tremble so?" Rani asked, placing a concerned hand on Kung's shoulder.

"Oh, Rani," said Kung, "there is danger of which I cannot speak. I can only say that this deed was done by the wizards who enslaved my uncle, and if their actions are not stopped, the entire empire may fall under their spell."

Kung knew exactly what must be done. Rani went to fetch his Unicorn, while Sari helped them pack food and supplies. Kung explained to his uncle that he had urgent business for the Emperor but would soon return.

Once at the South Gate of the city, Rani lifted Kung up behind him on his Unicorn. On the back of the fleetest beast in all the world, the two boys flew down the Spice Road. Riding by day and by night, they swept along like a racing wind. Although the wizards had started their journey southward three days before, Kung and Rani overtook them without their knowledge just the night before they had reached the Dragon Pass.

There Kung dismounted from the Unicorn. Stroking its soft nose, he thanked Rani for his steadfast friendship and

help. From here, he explained, only he could go on, for the dragon would surely slay them if they all attempted the pass without protection. And so, reluctantly, the boys parted, Rani returning to the Imperial City and Kung rushing toward Sung Wu to find the Master of the Sleeping Bamboo.

THE MESSAGE

KUNG BURST THROUGH the undergrowth and emerged at last in the clearing where he had spent his last evening with Panda in the Enchanted Valley. There Panda sat under his big tree, munching peacefully on a bamboo. Shang the Eagle Lord had told him of Kung's return some hours back, and he had come to the clearing to await the boy.

"Panda!" Kung cried in excitement. "I m-m-mean, my Lord Beishung...I have urgent news..."

"Now, now, young Kung!" Panda raised a paw for him to cease. "I am happy indeed to see you once again, but in civilized nations, such as China, we have certain beliefs in decorum. You must calm down, and we'll come to matters of import at their proper time. Now have a seat on the grass beside me. I can see you've had a difficult journey. Here, take this cup of honey tea with some fruit. A tangerine, perhaps? Now don't be impatient. Tell me, how is your uncle? Have you managed to win his freedom?"

Dutifully Kung told Panda of his uncle's release from slavery.

"Fine, excellent. You are a brave young man. Now tell me news of the Emperor and the state of the courts of the Imperial City."

Kung told of the spectacles of the court, his own

entrance into it, how he played his flute for them all. He spoke of how beautiful the Princess was. Then he told Panda of the Emperor's strange obsession: the Imperial Collection and how the Emperor, in his passion to collect every magical creature on earth, had offered his daughter as the reward for capturing the rarest and most magical of creatures.

"Which is *me*, of course!" concluded Panda cheerfully. "Well, well. So now the wizards must be on their way to hunt me down. Have you come to warn me of that?"

"Yes, yes, my Lord," began Kung, "except..."

"Well, thank you, young Kung, but you must not alarm yourself. In the Sleeping Bamboo the wizards could not gain power over me. Now, now, don't protest. What concerns me more is the foolishness of the Emperor. What kind of ambition is this for an emperor? He wants to become the greatest zoo-keeper in history? Nonsense! What are the emperors coming to these days?

"Why, Shen Nung, the Ancient One, who ruled seventeen generations, did not decide one day that he was to be the oldest emperor in *The Book of Histories*. Nor did the Yellow Emperor, Huang Tu, who tamed dragons and had a  great chariot towed across the sky, do so to become the best dragon-tamer in the world. Neither did the Great Yu, who changed the course of the rivers of the world, do so just for the fame. He desired only to save the people from a universal flood."

Kung grew fearful that if he didn't interrupt the Panda now, the wizards might descend on them any moment.

"But, Panda, I mean Lord Beishung, the wizards have the Fire Dragon's pearl, the terrible Black Pearl!" he exclaimed. "They mean to entrap you with it, or destroy you! You must flee!"

"The Black Pearl?" the Panda repeated a little absent-mindedly. "My goodness, do you mean *the* Black Pearl? From the Fire Dragon! Oooooh, that's a frightful pain. I can't say I like that in the least. They really are a nasty lot, these wizards, aren't they? I haven't seen worse since... oh, the Emperor Chin's time.

"Now Chin, of course, built that Great Wall, but he was a bit like our present Emperor. Let other things go to pot for one big project. Bandits about everywhere, wizards having their way..."

"But what are we going to do?" pleaded Kung.

"Do? Oh, my young Kung, you are always one for *doing* things, aren't you? I suppose that's in your nature," said Panda in what he hoped was an understanding tone. "Humans are rather like that, I suppose. However, you are right," he concluded resolutely. "What *you* must do is leave the Enchanted Valley at once. Go directly to your uncle's cottage and remain there until things clear up.

"Oh, don't worry, I'll have these wizards chasing me until they're exhausted. Even wizards get bored after a few weeks of chasing about the old bamboo forest, tripping over things, getting tangled up in thickets, tearing their robes, getting their amulets caught in the bushes, dropping their swords in mucky old swamps and what not.

"Not to worry, not to worry. Doing battle with the Panda is the worst thing in the world for wizards. A real nightmare," he said, chuckling. "It's what the Yellow Emperor used to call *Panda-monium*.

"Hmm, I wonder if wizard curses have changed in the last few hundred years or so. They were very nasty in the old days. Well, we shall see. Anyway, thank you very much, my boy. Now go off to your uncle's cottage and take that ring with you for safety's sake."

"But with my ring I could steal the Black Pearl," Kung suggested boldly. "I could just pick their pocket or something."

"Steal the Black Pearl!" Panda was appalled. "Good heavens, young man! I won't have you *steal* anything. And, furthermore, if you touch that nasty thing, it would burn a hole right through your hand and fall on the ground.

"Don't worry, I'll just let them thrash about until they're exhausted. And without me, they can't get the Princess for a prize. So off you go, and I'll be on my way to greet our guests," Panda said with a twinkle in his eye.

BATTLE OF THE WIZARDS

THUNDER ON A CLEAR DAY? When Kung awoke in his uncle's cottage, bright sunlight was streaming through the window but in the distance he could hear thunder.

Kung rolled out of bed and went to the window. He had slept for nearly two full days. He looked up into the sky and saw only the bright sun and blue heavens. But over the Enchanted Valley a dark cloud hovered above the tops of the trees and the bamboo. Flashes of lightning and thunder came out of this strange black cloud. At times the cloud was like a black dragon, then a panther, then a serpent. It was a deadly sight, crackling with fire. Kung had no doubt that this was the work of the wizards in their attempt to catch the Panda.

Truth to tell, it was just as well that Kung decided to obey the Panda's wishes and stay clear of the Enchanted Valley, for the battle was fierce. The wizards raged for days and days over all the valley. Curses and paralyzing spells were tossed about. Toran's magic sword struck down trees; Tu's fiery arrows shot through the bamboos; Tamba's exploding spears sent up columns of smoke. The frenzied wizards dashed about, leaping and shouting and knocking down the rhododendrons. Thinking they heard Panda in one clump of bamboo or blackthorn, they would blast away with all their might, only to hear Panda chuckling in another grove behind them. Furiously they pursued him day after day, falling into murky swamps, hidden pools, thorn thickets and groves full of spiderwebs, gadflies, mosquitoes and hornets. And while the fierce wizards trailed after him, Panda chuckled from another part of the Enchanted Valley.

Never in all their lives had the wizards suffered more at the hands of an enemy. And they hadn't even *seen* this enemy. They were wet and cold, covered in mud and stung by insects. They had torn their clothes, ruined their weapons, lost their amulets and were bleeding from cuts and bruises. With evening approaching, they collapsed in a heap in a part of the Sleeping Bamboo where they had blasted a clearing.

"A wizard's job is a dirty one," said Tu, the wizard with the bow and the shaved head, "but someone's got to do it." Tamba the Spearman grunted in assent. Toran said nothing. He was as exhausted and frustrated as the others, but his blue eyes were looking into some far-off place. Distantly he could hear the sound of music, a flute echoing in the hills beyond the Enchanted Valley.

"Of course," said the wizard, "it's the boy." The other wizards did not know what Toran was talking about. "The fluteplayer, Kung the shepherd boy. I can hear his flute. With him perhaps we can capture Panda! Come, listen to my plan..."

As Toran whispered, the others nodded and scowled. Then each got up and went into the forest in a different direction. Despite the darkness, they again began their noisy attack on the Panda. Their plan was to distract Panda while Toran slipped out of the valley and went on to Kung's cottage.

Toran the Swordsman was so stealthy that Kung did not wake even when the wizard crept to the boy's bedside. When Toran seized Kung with his strong hands, the boy did not even have the chance to take the magic jade ring from his necklace and slip it on his finger. The wizard took a short piece of rope and tied Kung's hands behind his back. Then he tossed Kung over his shoulder like a sack of rice and strode off toward the Sleeping Bamboo.

By dawn Toran was joined by his two companions in their blasted clearing. "Now it's our turn to laugh," said Toran, displaying his catch. And indeed he and Tu laughed heartily, while Tamba smiled and clapped his hands.

"Enough," said Toran fiercely. "We now have our business with the Panda." Then in a voice so loud and deep that it resounded through the Sleeping Bamboo, the Swordsman called out: "My Lord Beishung, we, the wizards of Zandu, bid you to come forth if you value the life of this lad. He is the one called Kung the Fluteplayer, the nephew of your friend Latzu."

Toran was holding Kung roughly by his collar as he called out to Panda, and the boy knew that his grip was far too strong to break. He did not try to struggle but he shouted desperately, "No, Panda, no! Do not come. Don't let them capture you."

The wizard clapped a hand over Kung's mouth.

At that moment someone called out from the forest. It was the Panda's gentle but commanding voice. It seemed to come from all parts of the clearing. "Do not harm the boy. I will come. First, untie him."

Toran untied the rope that bound Kung's hands behind his back but he held the boy's wrists firmly. "He is unbound," said Toran. "Come forth!"

On the far side of the clearing, in the shifting shadows of the bamboo, something moved. Then out of the shadows and patterns of the forest emerged the Panda.

Tears came into Kung's eyes as Panda walked slowly and fearlessly into the clearing. "Release the boy," he demanded, "and I will forfeit my freedom for his safety."

As Toran let go of Kung, with all speed the wizard reached into a pouch on his belt and pulled out something, throwing it on the ground before Panda.

Kung fled as fast as his legs would carry him. "I'm free!" he shouted as he headed into the bamboo. "Panda, run and save yourself."

But it was too late. For Toran had thrown the Fire Dragon's Black Pearl on the ground in front of the Panda. It lay malevolent and hypnotic, like a black evil eye with a flame flickering deep within. Its bottomless darkness drew the unfortunate Panda deeper and deeper down. He was in a trance from which he could not awaken. The possessors of the Black Pearl had him in their power.

The wizards shouted with joy. Laughing, they mocked the Panda who thought he was so clever. Now vast wealth would be theirs, and power as well. Through the capture of the Panda and the Emperor's foolishness, they would become the masters of the Celestial Empire.

THE WHIRLWIND

SOON AFTER the capture of Panda the wizards made ready to return to the Imperial City and lay claim to their reward. But Tu the Bowman was concerned about Kung. "What of the boy? Shall we hunt him down?"

"He can do us no harm and we would only waste time in the pursuit," said Toran. "He must have fled back to Sung Wu."

But even as the wizards spoke, Kung was peering at them through the bamboo. And Kung had no intention of fleeing to the safety of Sung Wu.

When the wizards were ready, Toran took the lead. Then the silent Tamba, who held the Black Pearl, was followed by the entranced Panda. Walking upright, leaning forward like a circus seal balancing a ball on the nose, Panda stared into the pearl which Tamba held aloft. The three were followed by Tu at the rear of this procession.

Despite the watchful Tu, Kung followed as closely as he dared through all the day. It was dusk before the wizards decided to halt the march. They would sleep one more night in the Enchanted Valley before facing the challenge of the Dragon Pass.

Finding another clearing, the wizards made their camp for the night. They again dropped the Black Pearl on the ground, and Panda sat back on his rump with a thump at the edge of the clearing. He stared in his trance. While the pearl was there, he could not blink or move.

The wizards built a fire and made themselves a fine meal. Then they drank their evil potions, sang songs of heroic wizards and told each other lies about their own conquests.

All this time Kung lay hidden in the bamboo, keeping himself alert long into the night while the wizards enjoyed themselves in their encampment.

Finally, as the embers of the fire died down, the last of the wizards dropped off to sleep. Kung slipped on the jade ring and stealthily crept into the clearing. Fearful that he might stumble or make some noise and wake the wizards, he moved ever so slowly toward the sleepers. One of the wizards stirred and even opened an eye, but the ring of invisibility saved Kung from being discovered. Boldly Kung crept up to each of the wizards and slipped the magical gold rings from their fingers.

Kung sighed in relief. Without their rings these evil men would not wake in the morning. In fact, thought Kung, they were so evil they would probably not wake for centuries. Kung gathered a pile of weapons, rings and evil amulets. He then removed his jade ring and sat for a time near the still-warm coals of the fire.

When dawn came he looked across the clearing at the Panda, who remained staring into the black depth of the evil pearl. Kung went over to the Black Pearl, but even at a distance of a few feet he could feel its heat. When he put his hand a few inches above it, it was like putting his hand over a flame.

Kung sat down in despair. What could be done? Panda could not be moved because the Black Pearl held him in a trance, and Kung could not move or even touch the evil pearl.

After a time Kung took out his flute and began to play. The gentle music calmed him and allowed him to think. Kung thought how Panda was the wisest being he had ever known. If he were Panda and Panda were him, what would he do now? What was it that the Great Panda had always said? *Balance, not conflict. Overcome evil with reason, not with force.*

Panda had said that in the time of chaos, before the world had order, the black pearls were the seeds of strife and the fire dragons ruled. But into that Abyss the Supreme-Being-of-the-Ninth-Heaven dropped white pearls of equal but opposite strength. If this were so, reasoned Kung, could it be that the White Pearl of the Ice Dragon might now neutralize the power of the Black Pearl of the Fire Dragon?

Quickly Kung stood up and went over to the sleeping wizards. He saw that Tu the Bowman carried a leather pouch identical to the one Toran had used for the Black Pearl. Kung took the pouch from Tu's belt and opening it, he saw the huge White Pearl of the Ice Dragon. Even in the pouch Kung could feel the iciness of the pearl and its phenomenal weight. Without touching it, Kung rolled the White Pearl out of the pouch onto the ground directly between the Black Pearl and the Panda.

At exactly that moment there was a clap of thunder. Wind sucked through the trees. The pearls confronted each other. They seemed to throb and glow. One was like a fierce black sun, the other a cold white moon. Then they began to move: they whirled about in a circle, faster and faster, until like two comets, one black and one white, they surged in a great whirlwind, sucking everything into the vortex. Kung leapt toward Panda, and wrapping his

legs about his tummy, he grasped the stout branch of a tree with his hands and hung on with all his might.

The pearls whirled on and on, finally rising into the heavens. The two magical pearls, the wizards' weapons, the rings, the robes, and finally even the wizards themselves rose up with the whirlwind and disappeared in the distant sky.

Only Kung and Panda remained. At last Kung released his grip on the tree and unwrapped his legs from around Panda's furry tummy. Then Panda stirred and blinked his eyes. He looked about, then lifted a paw and gently stroked Kung's hair.

"My, my," said Panda, as if he were simply awakening from a nap. "Life is so interesting, isn't it? Something new happens every century whether you're ready for it or not."

With a tear in his eye Kung looked at Panda's peaceful face; then hearing a deep chuckling coming from Panda's belly, the boy began to laugh too.

The Emperor's Panda

HE NEXT MORNING Panda rose early, as usual, and conjured up a meal of bamboo, rice, coconut milk and various exotic fruits laid out on his silk napkin. As Kung crunched on a pomegranate and Panda was busily peeling a bamboo shoot, Kung thought how peaceful it was once again in the Enchanted Valley. Now in the warm sunshine he could hardly believe the terrible battles of the last few days.

"Well," said Panda, breaking into the boy's thoughts, "where do we go from here? I mean, after breakfast and on for the next generation or so?"

Kung thought it was a rather large question, but Panda merely scratched his ear with a piece of bamboo and concluded, "I think I should go to the Emperor's court."

"Good heavens," said Kung in alarm. "They might throw you in some nasty cage and keep you locked up forever!"

"My dear boy, not now. Especially as you will be the one to take me to the Emperor's court and claim the hand of the Princess as your reward. With you as my keeper in such a high office, I think I can depend on fair treatment, don't you? We will dispense with cages altogether, as it was in the old days. I shall have my usual chamber in the court and come and entertain the Emperor and the palace officials in the great hall, as I did long ago."

"But...but...my Lord...." Kung was startled by Panda's decision. "I, a simple shepherd, marrying the Princess...."

Panda chuckled. "My dear Kung, you have proven yourself braver and wiser than anyone in the empire. It was you who learned the lesson of balance. Without violence and through wisdom, you saved the Celestial Empire from an age of darkness and sorcery.

"In any case, it's high time I returned to court again," said Panda. "It's been quite restful in the Enchanted Valley, but it's time I returned to the world for a while. Set everything straight in the empire. I mean, things have gone quite far enough, don't you agree?

"Yes, yes, of course you do," continued Panda before Kung could even open his mouth. "So, I *want* you to take me to the Emperor. You'll marry the Princess and then the two of us will manage quite well, don't you think? Get things in order. And we'll let the Emperor have his silly old zoo. I'll dance about and be the royal clown to amuse him. After all, the Emperor's not so bad. Rather harmless if we handle him properly. You'll see."

So off they went and not many days later they reached the Imperial City. News of their coming had preceded them, and they were greeted at the gate by Kung's uncle, Latzu, now fully recovered. There too was Rani, Sari, the Unicorn and the whole theatre troupe. Guardsmen and officials were present, and when the gates were thrown wide open there was celebration in the streets. A grand procession formed behind Kung and the Master Panda as they made their way to the palace. The Panda's return was an omen of such good fortune that all the city rejoiced.

When at last Kung and the Master Panda stood before the Emperor the old man smiled with pleasure. He announced there would be a week of feasting and celebration to mark this day. He knew now that his destiny had been fulfilled and that his place in history was secure.

At the Emperor's side the Princess Li Su sat upon her throne, her face betraying her own happiness. Her destiny and Kung's could now be as one.

True to the Emperor's promise, on the last day of the celebrations marking the return of the Panda there was a royal wedding. In the company of the Emperor and all the lords and ladies of the land, Kung's uncle and friends—and of course the Master Panda—Kung was married to the Princess Li Su.

When at last the Emperor grew too old to rule any longer, he turned to his people and asked, "And who should rule after me?"

"Is there not Kung?" they all replied as one.

Thus, Kung the Fluteplayer, shepherd from the forgotten land of Sung Wu, became Emperor of all China. To his court came scholars and poets, artists and actors, philosophers and sages. With his beautiful and wise Empress on one side, and the Master Panda on the other, and with his many allies and friends, Kung brought about a Golden Age of Enlightenment such as China had never seen.

In time Kung grew to be very old and wise, but the Panda remained as Kung had first known him. One day Panda and the aging Kung sat down in a courtyard beneath a banyan tree.

"The old Emperor was not such a foolish man after all," reflected Panda. "He knew he had a destiny to fulfil. He consulted the oracle of the jades and looked hard for that path. And the result of his grand contest was fortuitous for all, was it not?"

"But what a risk," said Kung.

"Yes, yes, a great risk—a terrible thing if the wizards had won. But they did not—by a hair's breadth. By the weight of a feather the scales were balanced by you, Kung. By such small measures the laws of heaven are upheld. And through these circumstances your time had come to be a power in the world," said Panda.

"A great and full time it has been," said Kung, "though it will soon pass."

"As with all mortals, the time will come for you to climb the jewelled stairs to the Heaven of Ancestors. And then, my dear Kung, my time too will have passed. I will ascend to the Ninth Heaven."

The Emperor Kung turned to Panda, much alarmed. He pleaded that he stay on and guide his children and their children. What would become of the world without the wisdom of the Panda?

"There is an age for everything," Lord Beishung explained patiently. "And both yours and mine must soon come to an end. I have much work to do in the Ninth Heaven.

"But do not despair. I do not abandon the world entirely, Kung. The time will have simply passed for the First Panda on earth. On the very night that I arise to the Ninth

Heaven, the stars will shine brightly on the bamboo forests of the empire. In the dark, secret places of those groves the starlight will awaken a whole race of sleeping pandas. Not immortal beasts, not gifted with all my magical powers, but in my image nonetheless. These children of the Master Panda will not be blessed with the gift of speech, and indeed in most ways they will be as other wild, gentle beasts. But if the people are willing to come for a time and sit quietly with the children of the Master Panda, I'm sure they will learn quite as much as the First Panda could teach the Emperor Kung. Don't you think so?" Panda's bright black eyes gazed fondly at Kung.

The Emperor Kung sat for some time under the tree with his friend and thought deeply. Then he smiled sadly and nodded.

And that is the end of the story of how Kung the Flute-player went on a great adventure and changed the destiny

of the Celestial Empire. Except for one thing—the insignia of Emperor Kung.

When Kung was made Emperor under the Panda's guidance, his first deed was to order an insignia—a seal of office to be placed on the banners of his palace and the offices of all his governors. This was not a grand insignia such as other emperors had made for them. It was a simple one, which looked like this:

Many thousands of years have passed since Kung was Emperor, and with wars and the burning of books, his name and deeds have been forgotten. But in all that time the great seal has survived. Even today the people throughout China look at the insignia that Kung made long ago and attempt to learn the lesson of balance and harmony.

But even in Kung's time the people wondered at its meaning. Some of the wiser guessed it must have something to do with the Master Panda. Perhaps it was the Panda rolled up and juggling two balls. Most understood the lesson of balance it conveyed, but there was nobody who guessed the truth of its origin. There was nobody who knew about the two dragon pearls—one black and one white—at the centre of two comets that pursued one another in the circle of a great whirlwind.

But perhaps this was how Kung and Panda planned it. After all, it's nice to have a secret that nobody else knows, isn't it? And as Panda himself might say: "Nobody knows *this* secret – well, *almost* nobody. There is *me*. And now, of course, there is *you*."

The End